Praise for *Airpl*

Short-Listed for the New Am
Long-Listed for the Andrew Carn ⸺ ⸺ ⸺ Excellence

"Now lands *Airplane Mode*, by Shahnaz Habib, a lively and, yes, wide-ranging book that interrogates some of the pastime's conventions and most prominent chroniclers . . . Habib [is a] ruthlessly honest and funny observer."
—Alexandra Jacobs, *The New York Times*

"These essays by an Indian writer and translator should be required reading for anyone who has trouble finding travelogues outside the canon of privileged white writers."
—Bethanne Patrick, *Los Angeles Times*

"The frequent fliers in your life are likely to be enlightened and entertained." —Michael Schaub,
The Orange County Register

"Insightful, funny, moving, politically astute . . . Habib's book is rich and her narrative voice analytic, historically informed, and passionate . . . Habib compels us to engage in the politics of travel." —Nalini Iyer, *International Examiner*

"Thoughtful and thought-provoking . . . It's both a welcome addition to the existing library of literature on travel and a resonant critique of much of it—and it may well leave you thinking more about your own experiences making your way across the globe." —Tobias Carroll, *InsideHook*

much of documentary and travel writing. This elegantly written, erudite collection acts not only as a much needed corrective but as an exemplar of what the travel essay can truly accomplish." —Hasanthika Sirisena, author of *Dark Tourist*

"*Airplane Mode* is a captivating and comprehensive history of travel. Part cultural study and part personal account, it engages with the troubling legacy of colonialism and the particular experiences of brown and Black people traveling. I know of no other book like it, a thrilling read that feels like a whole education in the history of why and how bodies moved across this not-so-lonely planet."
—Kazim Ali, author of *Northern Light*

"A fascinating, wide-ranging, and insightful travelogue that poses some of the biggest questions of all: who gets to travel and what is it that makes us so keen to travel in the first place?" —Annabel Abbs, author of *Windswept*

"I read *Airplane Mode* while traveling for work and was thrilled to find it reignited my love for travel memoirs. In interweaving the personal and political stakes of traveling as a migrant, Habib gives us an urgently needed reimagining of the genre." —Jessica J. Lee, author of *Two Trees Make a Forest*

"Nuanced and thought-provoking, *Airplane Mode* is an exemplary piece of work that asks important questions about our current concept of 'travel writing.' Shahnaz Habib expertly blends personal anecdotes with external research to interrogate typically romanticized ideas of travel and immigration, and how our personal definitions of those subjects change depending on, amongst other factors, the passports we are born holding. I will be recommending this book to anyone I know who's ever set foot on a plane, in another country, or has dreamed of a life of 'traveling'—so essentially, everybody."   —Pyae Moe Thet War, author of *You've Changed*

AIRPLANE
MODE

TRANSLATED BY SHAHNAZ HABIB

Jasmine Days by Benyamin
Al Arabian Novel Factory by Benyamin

AIRPLANE MODE

An Irreverent History of Travel

SHAHNAZ HABIB

Catapult
New York

First Catapult edition: 2023
First paperback edition: 2024

Hardcover ISBN: 978-1-64622-015-1
Paperback ISBN: 978-1-64622-239-1

Library of Congress Control Number: 2023936786

Cover design by Dana Li
Cover images: mountains © iStock / kwiktor;
bougainvilleas © iStock / MarsBars;
carousel © iStock / Mark Ronay;
plane icon © IronSV / Noun Project
Book design by Wah-Ming Chang

Catapult
New York, NY
books.catapult.co

Printed in the United States of America

1 3 5 7 9 10 8 6 4 2

For my family,

the diaspora on which the sun shall never set

Contents

AIRPLANE
MODE

Chapter

ONE

✈

THE HAGIA SOPHIA WAS A MUSEUM WHEN I MET MEGAN under its roof. Now it is a mosque again, after previous lives as an Orthodox church, a Catholic cathedral, and an Ottoman mosque. But this was 2007, and I was standing under its dome, trying to take in fifteen centuries of interior decoration, when a young white woman touched my arm: "Excuse me, may I borrow your guidebook?"

Megan was backpacking through a number of countries with a fat Europe guidebook that did not go into a lot of detail about every monument. So when she could, she would borrow guidebooks from other tourists. I offered her my *Lonely Planet Turkey* and she quickly scanned the section on the Hagia Sophia. A few hours later, we were drinking salep on the third floor of a nearby coffee shop.

Megan had set out from Amherst after a bad breakup that summer. She had started in Italy in June and now it was December in Istanbul, Europe's final, dubious outpost. She had a ticket to Bangkok in two weeks and she was thinking of doing Turkey in one week and then fitting in a little Iran before that. While minarets seemed to sway in the breeze outside our coffee shop's window, she ticked off Europe on her fingers. Bulgaria was still pretty. Albanian buses were not to be trusted. Don't choose between Madrid and Barcelona. In the two days that she had spent in Istanbul, she had already done Topkapi Palace, the Grand Bazaar, the ferry across the Bosphorus, and the museums. The most worthwhile ones, that is.

"What have you done so far?" she asked.

"This and that," I evaded.

I had been sleeping. No way could I admit this to Megan. But I had slept through every day since getting to Istanbul the week before. Waking up in the early evening, I would wander in circles in the market outside my hotel in an unfashionable neighborhood that happened to hold one of the cheaper hotels I found online. The market consumed me. The stacks of grape leaves and cabbage leaves. The animal carcasses hanging from hooks. The streetcar clanging its way through the middle of the road. A middle-aged man waited at the bus station with his elderly mother, his hands holding hers tenderly. Schoolchildren on their way home paused at the entrance of a tiny mosque for a quick mumbled prayer. A group of young women in high heels and headscarves sashayed by in a flutter of style and confidence and secrets. Eventually, I would find some unspectacular dinner in one of the nearby lokantas and return to my hotel room. I felt lonely and intimidated and depressed. It was all a far cry from the glamorous travels I had imagined when I booked my ticket for Istanbul.

Back home in New York, my roommate had told me that

she thought I was brave to travel alone in Turkey. "Those places are scary," she said. Walking through the market every day, I would often remember the shrug with which she had pronounced that and it would fill me with a kind of angry confusion. I thought then that it was because she was perpetuating the fearmongering stereotypes that Muslim countries are often portrayed with. But looking back now, I wonder if some of my confusion was also about my own inadequacy as a tourist. It was not just the fact that there was nothing remotely scary about this market; it was the contrast between her perception of me as "brave" and my own failure to live up to the adventurousness and intrepidity required of a good traveler.

This has happened to me again and again. In a new place, I am never adventurous; I am cautious. It takes me a few days simply to get used to stepping out of wherever I am staying. At first, I stick to the neighborhood, like an animal getting used to a new environment. I want to be curious and intrepid; instead, I am confused and lonely. (Jet lag does not help.) And always I am conscious of what a waste of time this is. If only I could just get up and go do things, how much time I could save. I am basically the opposite of Anthony Bourdain. Not cool, not adventurous. And vegetarian! As I walked around the market staring, asking in my feeble herbivorous voice, Etsiz yemek var mı?, I sensed each precious day in Istanbul turning like the pages of an unread guidebook.

For years I had dreamed of visiting Istanbul. Wanderlust codes our desires in different ways, and the software that ran underneath my own wanderlust for Turkey was programmed by my reading. I had started studying Sufi poetry a few years before and was part of a mosque community in New York that traced its lineage to a Sufi mystic from Istanbul. I loved the contradictions of this poetry, how the seeming sensuousness gave way to a rigorous self-inquiry.

In a related contradiction, the more I wanted to travel, the less I could, thanks to bureaucratic mysticism. For several years, I had been unable to leave the United States. My student visa had expired, and in this tricky position, I could continue to live in the United States legally, but if I left its borders, I could not return. This meant not returning to India and not seeing my family for four long years while I tried to switch to a different visa. An employment visa was out of the question in the kind of low-paid jobs I had a talent for finding. When I worked up the courage to ask the filmmaker whose office I was running if he would consider sponsoring my visa, he suggested that I should go to graduate school so I could get another student visa. One immigration lawyer suggested incorporating as a business and hiring myself. Another one misplaced my passport for a few days.

As I worked through my immigration troubles, I kept thinking of Turkey. I distracted myself from my immigration conundrums by reading Pamuk novels, only half understanding them. I was drawn to the geometric rhythms of ilahis and started learning Turkish. And then finally one day my new visa came through and I quit my job (which would have been dramatic if I had an actual job and not a bunch of vague freelancing arrangements) and booked my round-trip ticket to India with a stopover in Istanbul, and here I was.

When you read about a city, it is standing still, cryogenically frozen in an author's words. You pick up a guidebook and in its little guidebook prism, the city and all its history and culture are so neatly packaged for you. But when you are actually there, for instance, walking through the ancient Hippodrome, now a historic district teeming with backpackers, somebody will trample on your feet while taking a photo. Outside the Blue Mosque, office workers are eating lunch in the square with their backs turned to the building you have traveled halfway around the world to see. A young couple saying goodbye and lingering afterward will remind you that you are alone, that you have no one to share this journey with. Something melancholy in the city will poke you with an ice-cold finger and say, "Little tourist, you can have my palaces and minarets, but you cannot have me."

Many years later, I would return to Istanbul to live there for several months with my husband and daughter. The city would fall into perspective then, its neighborhoods mapping themselves into my memory, friendships blooming out of the rich soil of daily life. The translators and writers we worked with, fellow parents at the neighborhood school my daughter attended, the cranky musician who ran our favorite tea shop where each tea was named after a maqam, the fish restaurant where one of Istanbul's minor earthquakes shook our table. Alongside the ferries and palaces and mosques, we got to know the supermarkets and banks and minibus stops and lending libraries. Istanbul's monuments,

taken in small and regular doses, became beloved familiars
to me in those months. The neighborhood market days became my shopping days, not sights to see.

I am so tempted to tell you about that trip; it's much
cooler, more glamorous, easier to remember and relish. But
what are we to do with the confusion and loneliness of traveling? Leaving the monoculture of the United States and
landing in a nonchalantly multilayered and superbly hybrid
city like Istanbul can be overwhelming. Some places test us,
and traveling alone tests us, and my miserable first week
in Istanbul is more interesting to me now than the happier
times I have had in the city since then.

So there I was feeling a bit silly and a lot lonely when I
ran into Megan, intrepid and adventurous Megan, who had
already *done* so many monuments, though she had only
been in Istanbul for two days. I could not even have begun
to articulate the dull ache I felt. I was also intimidated by
Megan, who dared to walk up to strangers and ask to see
their guidebooks. Here I was losing myself in the shy silence
that surrounds a solo traveler, my breath turning stale from
lack of conversation, and there she was, stepping between
continents with practiced ease. And so, even though I had
a slight headache from hearing her talk—the beaches in
Croatia are still quite empty, Belgium has surprisingly good
coffee—I was delighted to listen.

And then she was gone. On the free map of Turkey that
she picked up from the Tourism Information Office, she
showed me her route, marked with arrows, and with the
directness of an arrow, she zigzagged through Turkey. We

promised to stay in touch; maybe our travels would inter-sect again.

It's difficult to describe the water-laced über-beauty of Istanbul's bridges and mosques and ferries without sound-ing like a tourist brochure for Las Vegas. It took me a week to see everything that Megan had seen in two days. This is not because I was a slow traveler, savoring every moment. In fact, I spent one whole day scrolling Facebook and send-ing friend requests to former coworkers because I started panicking that I would not have any work when I got back to New York.

Aghast at how much time I had wasted, I moved into the backpacker hostel Megan had stayed at. On my first morning there, in the breakfast room I found that the free bookshelf where other backpackers left behind books was crowded with Rumis and Pamuks. On the television in one corner, George Bush was making a Christmas speech to troops in Iraq. One of the breakfast servers said something funny and the others started laughing. I wanted to stay be-hind and find out what was said and why it was funny. But I felt the weight of my guidebook and all the sights I had not seen yet and so I left the warm breakfast room and the sound of laughter and walked to whatever mosque or palace it was that Lonely Planet thought I should see.

•

I wish I had known then that Karl Baedeker, the man who first popularized tourist guidebooks, died as the result of overwork at the age of fifty-eight. The man who systematized tourist trails so efficiently, at the very moment that leisure travel was transforming itself into a middle-class activity of cultural consumption, worked himself to death. When I came across this nugget of information years later, I understood so much about guidebooks and the particular ways in which they regulate the day of the tourist. Karl Baedeker founded the Baedeker publishing house in 1827, the year that also saw the launch of the first passenger-steamboat service on the Rhine. His eponymous "handbuchs" set the standard for travel guidebooks. Many of the conventions followed by the Lonely Planets and Rough Guides of today were either created or popularized by Baedeker, and after his death (of overwork, in case you forgot) his three sons expanded the company into multiple languages and continents.

Baedeker and another popular guidebook series that launched shortly after, Murray, soon became household names among European tourists. The books provided practical information on transportation and accommodation, detailed city maps, tables for steamboat fares, and guidance on foreign customs. All this information was arranged along numbered "routes" that extended from one large town to another. Baedeker also introduced the star system for must-see places. Beginning in 1844, Baedeker started awarding an asterisk to those points of interest that a cultured traveler must not miss at any cost. He would also inform his readers about what to safely ignore: "The Harbor [at Cannes] is unimportant"; "The view from the summit [at Mont Blanc] is unsatisfactory." In effect, he was creating a kind of Euro-tourism canon while also fashioning tourism into the act of seeing specific sights.

The most useful sentence I read about Baedeker comes from Edward Mendelson, who wrote: "Baedeker's science was first of all classical and Baconian." Francis Bacon's seventeenth-century articulation of man as the interpreter of nature and inductive reasoning as the most accurate path to a scientific truth is at the heart of the European Enlightenment ideal of knowledge, including the particular ways in which knowledge was captured by Baedeker's guidebooks. In the Enlightenment worldview, science and travel were deeply bound together. *Novum Organum*, the book Bacon published in 1620, depicts on its title page a ship sailing through the Pillars of Hercules, the legendary promontories, one on the European side and the other on the North African side, that flank the entrance of the Strait of Gibraltar. By choosing this image as the metaphor for his new scientific method, Bacon is signaling that he, too, is an explorer, like Columbus and Magellan, who went past the limits of the known world and navigated into the unknown represented by the Atlantic Ocean.

What the Baconian method does not take into account is the observer's subjectivity. Instead, it concerns itself with the phenomenon under investigation and takes the observer's objectivity for granted. Underlying this assumption is the notion that the observer is superior to the observed. Mendelson writes that Baedeker was scarcely alone in assuming that the observing Northern European was the most superior form of humanity. Famously in his note on "Intercourse with Orientals," Baedeker wrote: "Many are mere children, whose waywardness should excite compassion rather than anger, and who often display a touching simplicity and kindliness of disposition." While such extreme prejudices have mostly been weeded out of guidebooks, the Baconian understanding of the world as a subject to be observed by an objective European male observer for the benefit of other European males has continued well past the nineteenth century. Even today, guidebooks such as Lonely Planet and Rough Guides tend to assume a young Western backpacker as their Platonic-ideal reader.

I have a Baedeker. It's a 1904 edition of *Italy, from the Alps to Naples.* It used to belong to my mother-in-law, who inherited it from her grandfather. It's compact and fits neatly into my hand the way contemporary guidebooks don't, because the print is tiny. Bound in four sections that can be detached for the traveler's convenience, it is designed for "the use of those travellers who are obliged to compress their tour into a space of four or five weeks." It suggests that the traveler take rooms facing south in order to avoid drafts when possible and cautions against the growing rapacity and insolence of the lower classes of Naples.

And yet, it's also oddly moving. While it universalizes the male European point of view, the Baedeker also de-mocratizes travel information. Starting in the second half of the nineteenth century, as more middle-class and then working-class Europeans started traveling, they needed the Baedekers to tell them where to go and what to see. My 1904 Baedeker has a glossary that goes from *Affricano* (a dark variegated marble . . . from Greece) to *Villa*. There is something egalitarian about its pronunciation guide to Italian. The Baedeker knows that the person browsing its pages and testing out the Italian words is not on a Grand Tour.

•

The Grand Tour, a journey undertaken by young British nobles between the sixteenth and eighteenth centuries, marked the end of childhood and a transition into the social and cultural life of aristocracy. Traveling with an entourage of tutors and domestic servants for as long as two or three years, a duke or baron would begin the tour in England and go on to France and Italy. Rome, as the high-water mark of European civilization, was the ultimate destination. By the beginning of the nineteenth century, the Grand Tour had become entrenched as a rite of passage for young European elites. But with the sudden increase in disposable income brought about by the Industrial Revolution, as more commoners and women joined the ranks of travelers, the very nature of travel changed. Guidebooks enabled people who did not have access to cultural capital through breeding and education to enjoy the ruins of Rome. The Baedekers and Murrays came out of this moment of cultural ferment. Recreational travel was no longer the exclusive entitlement of gentlemen with personal Latin tutors. This also meant that Baedekers were looked down upon by more cultured travelers.

"Tut, tut! Miss Lucy! I hope we shall soon emancipate you from Baedeker. He does but touch the surface of things.

As to the true Italy—he does not even dream of it," Lucy Honeychurch is told by a fellow tourist, the adventurous Miss Lavish, on her first morning in Italy.

Lucy, the protagonist of E. M. Forster's 1908 novel, *A Room with a View*, is traveling in Florence with her chaperone and her Baedeker when we first meet her. Lucy is a terrific protagonist, a bit of a snob by nurture but kind by nature, perfect material for Forster's delicate irony. Her internal contradictions make great material for a novel that explores the moonwalking between class and gender, especially in the initial part of the novel, which takes place in the ambiguous foreign spaces offered by tourism.

Every time I pick up a guidebook, Lucy Honeychurch and Miss Lavish fight for my soul. Luckily we now have disembodied digital guidebooks and audio walking guides, which conceal themselves adroitly while murmuring information into our ears, like a politician's assistant at a fund-raising dinner. The human desire to not be caught with a guidebook while also miraculously enjoying all the information in a guidebook is approximately two centuries old. And the gentle art of shaming your traveling companion for looking at a guidebook is also just as old. After mocking Lucy for carrying a Baedeker, Miss Lavish takes her on a rambling walk through Florence, only to abandon her in the piazza outside Santa Croce.

It is true that guidebooks circumscribed the history and architecture and the arts and engineering of a place into a few pages, but this circumscribing was also an opening. Guidebooks offered their wisdom freely to those who had no opportunities to study or money to hire guides and tutors for lengthy travels abroad. Unfortunately, Lucy finds herself alone inside the basilica, without a Baedeker and too embarrassed to ask for help. It is then that she runs into a couple of fellow tourists from her pension, the Emersons, father and son. The son will offer, "If you've no Baedeker, you'd better join us." The story ends of course with Lucy marrying him.

It's not that Lucy needs her Baedeker to tell her how to feel. My favorite moment in the book takes place after she loses Miss Lavish and before she is found by the Emersons, when "the pernicious charm of Italy worked on her, and, instead of acquiring information, she began to be happy." Lucy is certainly capable of feeling the mystique of Santa Croce without her Baedeker, but how will she find her way back? How will she, a young woman abroad for the first time, learn to trust herself as a traveler? She is constantly surrounded by reproaches and cautions. She is told not to loiter, and she is expected to be ladylike.

Guidebooks such as the Baedekers may only touch the surface, but the surface is a good starting point for those who have only just been allowed to surface in the history of travel. Granted, guidebooks peddle in the banal. And yet who are we if we are not banal? Consider that the word *banal* itself has its etymological roots in medieval mills and ovens that were available for serfs to use and hence were commonplace, trite, ignoble. At the end of the book, when Lucy, instead of running away to Greece as she was planning, decides to marry George Emerson, I wondered how

Lucy's life would have turned out if she had her Baedeker that morning in Santa Croce. What if she could have enjoyed the solitary wandering opportunity that had unexpectedly visited her? The room with a view did not lead to a room of her own.

•

Guidebooks and the ways in which they classified cultural geography became handy for an unexpected audience in the twentieth century. In 1942, the German air force used *Baedeker's Great Britain* to target and bomb the historically famous cities of Exeter, Bath, Norwich, and York in retaliation for the Royal Air Force's blitzing of Lübeck. This kind of curious intimacy between guidebook knowledge and military information comes up again and again in guidebook history. Arthur Frommer, an army-intelligence lawyer posted to Berlin in 1955 during the Korean War, wrote *The G.I.'s Guide to Traveling in Europe* to share all the deals he found during his travels around the continent. In 2003, Jay Garner, the first U.S. administrator of occupied Iraq, used a Lonely Planet guide to draw up a list of historical sites that should be secured—while dropping 29,199 bombs on the country.

Today Lonely Planet, established by Tony Wheeler and his wife, Maureen, in 1973 after they backpacked across Asia and wrote up their tips as a book, is the Baedeker of our own times. Roughly one in four guidebooks sold today is a Lonely Planet. Originally intended as a countercultural travel companion, the Lonely Planets of the 1970s and '80s were intended to help shoestring backpackers to make their way through the Third World.* The first Lonely Planet was *Across Asia on the Cheap*, soon to be followed by "on the cheap" guides to Southeast Asia, Africa, and India.

In his *New Yorker* profile of Lonely Planet founder Tony Wheeler, Tad Friend wrote about these early iterations of the guidebook: "They advocated what might be called a playground model of behavior: here's the score on Lebanese grass and Balinese mushrooms, here's where to buy carpets in Iran before child-labor laws drive up the price, here's how to sell blood in Kuwait to pay for the rugs." The timely collapse of the Soviet Union (*Eastern Europe on a Shoestring*) and the deregulation of the airline industry helped Lonely Planet grow rapidly. But after 9/11 and the recession in the tourism industry, the company started deliberately broadening its audience, toning down the rebellious editorial voice to cater to a wider demographic, from global nomads to mature adventurers. Today it is a multinational behemoth with a massive online presence and a variety of allied businesses, from children's books to language guides. "Like Apple and Starbucks and Ben & Jerry's, all of which began as plucky alternatives, Lonely Planet has become a mainstream brand," Friend wrote.

Lonely Planet institutionalized the backpacker trail as we know it today, but this trail didn't come out of nowhere.

---

* See page 259.

On that first fateful trip across Asia on the cheap, Tony and Maureen Wheeler were following the Hippie Trail, which, in turn, was based on the "overland route" between Europe and Southeast Asia that had been used by colonial travelers as they toured around the colonies. In the postcolonial era, as different countries began managing their own railways, the overland route gave way to the Hippie Trail, which was best symbolized by the "magic buses" that picked up hippie travelers around Europe and sputtered and shuddered their way to Istanbul. There, the magic buses picked up a fair share of Americans as well as Australians and New Zealanders. Many of the travelers on the Hippie Trail were in search of Eastern mysticism, which they saw as an antidote to Western materialism. From Istanbul, the Hippie Trail found its way to South India or Southeast Asia, passing through Turkey, Iran, Pakistan, India, and then north to Nepal or south toward Goa and Kerala.

The trail connected a series of places that were remote and cheap—but remote for whom, and cheaper than what? Though the geopolitical tensions of the seventies changed the tenor of these travels, by the nineties, the backpacker trail was a well-beaten path in whose comfortable grooves young and adventurous white people met other young and adventurous white people. Backpacker hostels mushroomed along the trail, and banana pancakes started appearing on the menus of guesthouses in the Third World, from Chiang Mai to Goa.

Other parts of the world also developed their own trails. After the backpacker Yossi Ghinsberg got lost in the Amazon and was rescued, he wrote a book about his experience. Soon enough, a backpacker trail developed along the very places where he got lost. Pegi Vail's documentary *Gringo Trails* shows how many of the Indigenous men who helped rescue Ghinsberg now work as porters and local guides in this specific ecosystem. A Hummus Trail has developed in India over the last thirty years as Israeli backpackers started traveling to the beaches of Goa and the mountains of Kasauli to blow off steam after their compulsory military service. The increasing bilateral friendship between the right-wing Modi government and the Israeli government, built on a mutually beneficent arms trade, has certainly helped pave the bricks on that trail in recent years.

•

The next stop on my own not-so-grand tour and not-so-gringo trail was Konya. After a few more days of sleepwalking through Istanbul, I stirred myself enough to take a bus to this town in southeastern Turkey, where Mevlana Jalaluddin Rumi lived and died in the thirteenth century. Situated in the middle of the vast Anatolian heartland of Turkey, Konya was the eleventh-century capital of the Sultanate of Rum. By the time a young Sharia scholar called Jalaluddin, what we would now call an Afghan refugee, settled there with his family in 1228, Konya was a cosmopolitan center of Islamic learning whose madrassas were filled with the smartest philosophers and theologians. Jalaluddin would become the most renowned of them all, earning the title of master-teacher—Mevlana. It was Mevlana's encounter with Shams of Tabrizi, a wandering mystic, that inspired him to write the humanistic religious poetry that would come to be known around the world. The sacred wittiness of medieval Sufi poetry was a subterranean force in the Muslim spiritual and literary imagination long before it became popular among wellness gurus and neoliberals invested in "good Muslims." I first read about Al Hallaj and Mevlana Jalaluddin Rumi and Hafez in my mother tongue, Malayalam, when I stole my mother's copy of Vaikom Muhammad Basheer's essays.

A friend at my New York mosque had told me about a Sufi lodge near Mevlana's tomb, and as soon as I got to Konya, I went and knocked on their door. It was winter and I was the only lodger. I burrowed into the bed, piling bedspreads on top of me. Where Istanbul had poked me with a cold finger, Konya embraced me with soft sheepskin blankets. It was off-season and, like me, the town was sleepy. I learned to light the iron soba in the corner of my room without singeing my hair. The brothers who ran the lodge had a store nearby, filled with carpets, lamps, books, clothes, and prayer beads. In the back of the shop, there was always a soba glowing red and orange like a miniature sun. The sagging couch next to the soba was perfect for whiling away the afternoon reading.

Every now and then, the silence would be broken by Enis Abey, an old man from the neighborhood who would stop at the shop to warm his hands at the soba. Enis Abey adopted me. Though we couldn't speak more than two or three words in each other's languages, he would gather me on his walk through the town to go pluck some grass at the graveyards or to buy burek from the bazaar. Or we would share the sagging couch and Enis Abey would sing ilahis in his tender quavering voice.

I stopped counting the days I was spending in Konya. My days moved to the soft rhythm of an ilahi. I slept in, stopped by the store, and went on walks around Konya. The sun set early and the city was dark by four o'clock. In the afternoons, I returned to my room to write for four or five hours. Despite how little I did, there was so much to write about: The bazaar, with its maze of little shops selling oranges and jewelry and pistachios and steel locks and plastic buckets. The cemetery, where Enis Abey wept each time as he said goodbye, again, to long-gone friends and family and teachers. And the quiet centuries-old silence of Rumi's tomb.

The very next year, UNESCO would confirm the "Mevlevi Sema ceremony" of Turkey to be one of the Masterpieces of the Oral and Intangible Heritage of Humanity. When I returned to Konya several years later, the softness of the historic quarter was gone. The bazaar in front of Rumi's tomb where I bought bureks for dinner every day was replaced by a mega parking lot. So many of the tiny stores whose vendors entertained me out of sheer boredom had disappeared. One of those was Mehmet, who ran a carpet store behind the bazaar.

I met Mehmet on my second or third day in Konya. Mehmet had a store full of carpets but very little interest in selling them. All day he sat on a pile of carpets and conversed with whoever stopped by. We smoked my cigarettes and drank his apple tea, and he told me about the peasant women in Antalya who wove carpets from dawn to dusk and the U.S. soldiers from the nearby NATO base who came to check out his carpets.

It struck me as an incongruous detail back then—the soldiers shopping for souvenirs. The kind of detail whose jagged contours didn't quite fit the story I was trying to find in Konya. But years later, it fell into place, like a missing piece in a jigsaw puzzle, when I came across the word *militourism* in the poet Teresia Teaiwa's essay about how colonial forces were instrumental in constructing the Pacific islands as tourist paradises. Teaiwa describes how U.S. military and paramilitary forces circle the Pacific Ocean, ensuring the smooth running of the tourist industry, which returns the favor by helping to disguise the colonial and neocolonial aspirations of those forces. This symbiosis takes on many different shapes, from soldiers on R and R to tourists visiting war sites. Turkey too has its share of world-war sites, and many of the Australian backpackers I met in the hostel in Istanbul were heading to Gallipoli, the site of a major failed Allied campaign. The Gallipoli campaign marked Australia's entry into the war and is deeply embedded in Australia's national mythology. And, certainly, it helps that Lonely Planet, which is headquartered in Australia, has marked out Gallipoli as a must-see site.

"Where are you from?" Mehmet asked me the first time we met.

"Hindistan," I said, using the Turkish word for India.

"But you don't live in Hindistan," Mehmet guessed.

"How do you know?" I asked.

"Because you are traveling around. Only Americans, British, Australians, and Japanese travel." He ticked off the nationalities on his fingers.

In my first year in graduate school, I attended a job talk by a travel videographer who wanted to hire a crew for making travel documentaries. At some point his PowerPoint presentation delved into the travel habits of different demographics. "Europeans travel in August," "cruises are for retired Americans," "families with children rarely travel for more than a week," etc. And then he put on the final slide, the punch line: "People from the Third World do not travel; they immigrate."

Having spent a good many days of my life at various consulates, persuading visa officials that I did not wish to immigrate, merely to travel, I was especially stung by that. But when Mehmet said the same thing, I started laughing. He was not mocking me. Brown people like him and me did not fit the stereotype of the tourist. We were supposed to be the local color, the carpet sellers and flower vendors and guesthouse keepers. I thought then of Megan, her energy that confounded me, her easy charm with strangers, her ability to condense entire countries into crisp little sentences. How intrepid you are as a traveler depends, at least partly, on how entitled you feel to travel. On whether there's an army base nearby with soldiers from your country. On whether guidebooks are written to ease your path through the world.

I did not feel entitled to global travel in the same way that Megan did. The world did not feel mine. And as much as I resented the easy confidence with which Megan and the many white backpackers I had met on travels like these moved through the world, I could not resent them. I mean I could, but it felt false. Here I was traveling by myself, safe and sound and happy in a place I had dreamed about. I felt like fortune's spoiled child to be held in Konya's warm embrace. Besides, I knew that Megan's travels were not as easy as they looked. I knew she too felt the immense loneliness and wariness of women traveling solo, the way dangers seemed to lurk everywhere. It wasn't Megan's fault that I did not feel entitled to the world. And perhaps the word *fault* and the hermeneutics of faulting is the wrong way to approach this inequity. I did not want to feel entitled to the world. I did not want guidebooks to center me and my point of view. What kind of a way is that to get to know the places we go to? I did not want the invisible privileges that put a veil between me and the world.

We are primed to think of lack of privilege as a deficit. And of course it is that, in many big and small ways dictated by structural inequalities. But the more we think of it as a hole, the less whole we become. It is as if there are privilege-shaped holes in our selves—here is the hole where your white privilege should be, here is the hole where your straight privilege should be, here is the hole where your male privilege should be, here is where your able privilege should be, here is where your class privilege should be, here, here, here, and so on until some of us are mostly made of holes. But what if, instead of being a hole in the self, lack of privilege is more of a crack through which the light gets in? A third eye that reveals the magic-mushroom hybridity of the world we live in?

•

There's an Agatha Christie novel, published in 1944, about a woman called Joan Scudamore who has to spend a miserable week by herself waiting for a train at the Iraq border. Joan is a smug, middle-aged English woman whose world has revolved around her comfortable and respectable life with her lawyer husband and three children. After visiting her daughter and son-in-law in Baghdad, where the couple are part of the British colonial machinery, on her way back, Joan gets stuck in a rest house just outside the Turkish border because of bad weather. She is all alone and, while waiting for the next train, she reluctantly takes long walks in the desert every day. Little gestures and overheard conversations come back to her. Slowly, it dawns on her that she has bulldozed everyone in her life into living on her terms. Using all the marvelous skills that helped her create tight mystery plots, Christie creates a fascinating psychological novel with an unreliable narrator who becomes more reliable as she sits in the desert thinking about her life: the husband who she forced into a job he hated; her daughter who chose a husband in Baghdad because she wanted to get away from Joan's meddling; various friends that Joan considers condescendingly but then realizes they pity her loneliness.

It dawns on Joan that she has built a successful life by never considering anybody else's point of view. By the end, Joan realizes that no one actually likes her.

The novel is clunky and misogynistic, but Joan Scudamore is a good metaphor for the racialized white experience: how to deprive your soul by centering yourself constantly. Joan manages to make her life easy and comfortable but at the cost of seeing the world for what it actually is. Privilege is a stumbling block between the privileged person and the world. It takes away political and cultural proprioception from its wearer. What a shame to go through life like that.

Joan Scudamore is also interesting to me because she is authored by none other than Agatha Christie, champion of conservative British values and preservation of social mores through crime detection. Christie spent years in Syria, Iraq, and Turkey accompanying her second husband, the renowned archaeologist Max Mallowan, on his digs. The detective novels she set in Egypt and Iraq are fascinating cultural texts of British engagement in the Middle East in the interwar period. I have especially enjoyed tracking the Indian characters in these Middle East novels of Christie's. The rest house that Joan Scudamore is trapped in is run by an Indian man. One day in a desperate bid to keep away intrusive thoughts, Joan tries to talk to him:

> When the Indian came in to clear tea away
> she said to him:
>   "What do you do here?"
> He seemed surprised by the question.

"I look after the travelers, Memsahib."

"I know." She controlled her impatience. "But that doesn't take you all your time?"

"I give them breakfast, lunch, tea."

"No, no. I don't mean that. You have helpers?"

"Arab boy—very stupid, very lazy, very dirty—I see to everything myself, not trust boy. He bring bath water—throw away bath water—he help cook."

"There are three of you, then, you, the cook, the boy? You must have a lot of time when you aren't working. Do you read?"

"Read? Read what?"

"Books."

"I not read."

"Then what do you do when you're not working?"

"I wait till time do more work."

It's no good, thought Joan. You can't talk to them. They don't know what you mean. This man, he's here always, month after month. Sometimes, I suppose, he gets a holiday, and goes to a town and gets drunk and sees friends. But for weeks on end he's here. Of course he's got the cook and the boy . . . The boy lies in the sun and sleeps when he isn't working. Life's as simple as that for him. They're no good to me, not any of them. All

the English this man knows is eating and
drinking and "Nice weather."

I realize it doesn't quite make sense to blame the main
character of a piece of fiction for having Main Character
Syndrome, but it is also oddly fruitful to read between the
lines of books such as this to glimpse the alternative histories
that didn't get written down. It's fascinating to me that even
as Christie is meticulously creating her unreliable narrator,
she is, like many British travelers and writers of her time,
an unreliable narrator to the world she is moving through.
How little she sees of the sovereignty and agency that this
Indian man—in every way, her fellow traveler—must have.
How easily she decenters him and puts stereotypes into his
mouth so that her middle-class British character can continue to navel-gaze. When I imagine the enterprise and
energy that it must have taken for an Indian emigrant to
be running a guesthouse near Mosul in the 1930s, I am so
eager to read that story. Who was he? What part of India
was he from? How did he get there? What was it like to run
a guesthouse in 1930s Iraq, a newly independent nation
already being ripped apart by ethnic tensions exacerbated
by colonialism? I want that story, written on the margins of
colonialism.

What is a margin, after all? From the point of view of
the center, the margin is a faraway thing; it is where a space
ends. But where one space ends, another space begins. And
so the margin of one space is always the center of two different spaces. The margin, the border, the periphery is the line

along which spaces and peoples and things meet and mix. The margin begs from the center and borrows from next door and steals from itself. The margin is where the self gets to know itself.

•

In Tad Friend's 2005 profile of the Lonely Planet founders, he accompanies the Wheelers on a trip to Oman. Friend observes that every single hotel and restaurant is staffed by Indians. This is not a travel pattern that began in recent years. It harks back to the Indian Ocean maritime trade in the days before nation-states. It was reinforced by the British, who carried servants and soldiers from their Indian empire around their colonies. Today, the South Asian diaspora is all over the world in ways that belie the absence of South Asians from travel narratives. I have made it a game to spot the silent-but-enterprising brown people in the background of white travel narratives.

This is also what is missing for me in guidebook descriptions of the world outside the United States and Europe: a point of view that takes for granted the hybridity and multi-temporality of the world. As much as I love the sense of possibility that a Lonely Planet or a Rough Guide fills me with, I am also aware that I have to read these texts keeping in mind that I am not the readership they are intended for. The language in these guidebooks describes the world as it looks from the affluent monocultures that white tourists emerge from, a world in which *colonial* means *quaint*.

Minal Hajratwala, who updated the tenth edition of the
Moon Guide to Fiji, is one of the small minority of guidebook writers of color. Hajratwala, whose family diaspora
includes Indian immigrants in Fiji, was horrified by the dehumanizing language used in previous editions to describe
the island's people. For instance, in a section about hikes, the
ninth edition refers to the "fierce Lovoni tribe," who threat-
ened a town for decades. Conveniently omitted was the fact
that the town was a military outpost and the Lovoni people
were fighting to resist being captured and sold. Hajratwala
reframed this history in a section titled "Human Traffick-
ing of the 1800s," crediting the people of the Lovoni valley
for their resistance and explaining the history of colonial
kidnapping and selling of Pacific peoples. Imagine all the
guidebooks that need such re-visioning.

Pretty much every guidebook I have read for any Third
World country will describe it as a tapestry of cultures or
a colorful mix of ancient and modern. If more than half
the world is a mix of ancient and modern, perhaps then we
should accept that this particular hybridity is the norm,
while the vapid industrial modernity of a Western suburb is
the exception. If this constant and complex mixing of cultures is the real world, then why do guidebooks still lead
us on wild-goose chases for the "authentic"? No one is as
anxious about authenticity as a white tourist who rightly
suspects that the world has been watered down for their
benefit. But authenticity is a moving target; it has a talent
for confounding the search. Perhaps the solution then is to
understand and embrace the multiple hybrid shapes and

forms authenticities can take within the limitations of the tourism project.

•

Mehmet loved leafing through my Lonely Planet guidebook. One day he did a dramatic reading of the Konya section for his cousin who was visiting. "Konya is a conservative city, and travelers would be well-advised to dress modestly," he read, and then both of them burst out laughing. The cousin lived in a village near Kayseri that was famous for its carpets and had brought along a bunch for Mehmet to sell. He was looking forward to partying in Konya's nightclubs. "Just get out of this neighborhood," he told me, gesturing with his hands and sending cigarette smoke furling all over the shop. "This is not Konya."

The carpet shop, Rumi's tomb, my guesthouse—we were all in the historic district. Like many cities that depend on tourist income, Konya had gone to great lengths to preserve the neighborhood around its primary monument, the tomb where Mevlana Jalaluddin Rumi lay sleeping, serenely unaware that he was a bestselling twenty-first-century author. But outside the small radius of this neighborhood was a busy and thriving city. One day in search of a calendar for the new year, I walked down Aladdin Caddesi, the central avenue, which connects the medieval quarter of Konya with the more modern side of the city. It was disorienting after the days I had spent wandering around the historic quarter. I felt dizzy, as if I had stepped off a carousel. Mosques and bazaars gave way to ice cream parlors and stationery shops and parks and hardware stores and banks. It reminded me of my hometown, Ernakulam, in South India, and how it buzzes with the electricity of contemporary life while supplying made-in-China souvenirs and frozen fish to the former colonial quarter of Fort Kochi. I hadn't realized that there were so many universities in and around Konya. The streets were full of university students in a range of clothing that ran the gamut from modest to revealing, sometimes both at once. Of course they did not hang out in the historic district. Why would cool young people want to spend their evenings near the tomb of a dead thirteenth-century poet?

Another day, a new friend took me to dinner in his sister's house. It was in an apartment building in the suburbs of Konya, full of tall apartment buildings with lawns and children's playgrounds. As the car turned into the gated community compound where she lived, I felt disappointed. How could this medieval Sufi town have something as boring as a gated apartment community? And if Konya was actually this other Konya, then what was the point of only seeing the part that had frozen in time? I hardly knew Konya either, I realized grimly. I, too, had conveniently orientalized Konya, and how easy Konya had made it for me to orientalize.

That's when Megan's email arrived in my inbox. "Greetings from Goreme. After I left Istanbul, I went to Gallipoli, Izmir, Bursa, Ephesus, Antalya, and now am in Goreme. Are you going to meet me in Goreme?"

In Istanbul, on the green lawn in front of the Blue Mosque, there were always fat cats sleeping in the winter sun. From time to time, they would turn on their sides languidly. But then the call for prayer would ring out through the courtyard and the other mosques would echo it and the cats would leap away, as if ashamed of themselves. When Megan's email arrived asking if I would make it to Goreme, I felt like one of those cats that had wasted the afternoon sleeping, thinking tail-chasing questions like *How Konya is Konya if Konya is not Konya?* How to tell Megan that weeks after I should have left, I was still wandering around Konya?

"I have to go to Goreme," I told Mehmet glumly the next day.

"Yes," he agreed. "You are supposed to be traveling, seeing places, expanding your horizons."

"I cannot just spend the rest of my life in Konya."

"That would be no good."

"I could go tomorrow. There is nothing left for me to do here."

"Nothing at all."

"I will buy a bus ticket this afternoon."

"Wait, have you been to Meram?"

Meram, it turned out, is a village on a hill outside Konya. Legend has it that one day, Rumi and his disciples heard the sweet sound of the rebap wafting over to them from Meram. They were told that an Indian fakir who longed to be near Rumi had traveled all the way to Konya and was now living in a house in the hills of Meram. The fakir came to be known as Tavuz Baba because he befriended and fed the peacocks that lived in the Meram hills (*tavuz* is Turkish for *peacock*). Every day he would play the rebap and Rumi and his dervishes would whirl to his music without ever seeing him. His old house on the hill eventually became a mosque adjoining his tomb after he died.

"You are right. I will visit Tavuz Baba. I'll go to Meram tomorrow and Goreme the day after that," I decided.

I loved the stories about Rumi's dervishes. Before he was a poet, Rumi was a sheikh, a Sufi teacher and a scholar of law who had spent years learning Islamic fiqh. His disciples came from far and wide, and many sacrificed their lives to be his students. Many of them lived and died in and around Konya, and many of the city's residents speak of them as if they were eccentric grandparents. "Remember when Atish Baz Veli put his feet in the stove because there wasn't enough wood to cook the Mevlana's dinner?" They talk as if this happened within living memory, not seven centuries ago.

That evening, Enis Abey stopped by my lodge to pick me up on his way to a sema. Often referred to as the whirling dervish ceremony, sema is a form of moving meditation. It literally means *listening*. As the dervishes listen to the Beloved, they spin on their feet, turning constantly toward their hearts. Turning and turning and turning, with one hand lifted toward the sky to receive celestial blessings and the other hand seeking the earth to ground those blessings. Every Thursday, Enis Abey and some other dervishes in Konya assembled for sema in one of the local mosques.

In 1925, as part of an ambitious program of modernizing Turkey and secularizing its traditions, Mustafa Kemal

Atatürk banned all Sufi orders, including the order of Sufi dervishes that Rumi's son founded, the Mevlevis. Many Sufi orders went underground, meeting in stealth to practice the sema. In the 1950s, a visiting U.S. army official's wife asked to see a whirling dervish performance, sending Konya's authorities into a panic. William Dalrymple wrote in *The Guardian* of how the mayor eventually dug up an old dervish who was persuaded to teach the local basketball team how to whirl. Soon a whirling dervish performance became a fixture at the Konya sports hall during tourist season. Today you can catch such performances all over Turkey. But technically, the sema is still banned. Many Sufi orders that practice the sema as prayer prefer to keep a low profile.

We picked up some fruit from the market and went to the mosque. Unlike the many grand mosques I had seen in Turkey, this mosque was a simple affair, a house that you might pass by on the street. Enis Abey's fellow dervishes were already seated in a circle on the floor in the center of the living room. Harsh fluorescent lighting beamed down on them. All the windows were shut and barred. A group of musicians sat on one side and as we walked in, the ney player, who was blind, turned to us and smiled with eyes that didn't see but ears that could sense every rustle and every breath. Enis Abey joined the circle while I made my way to sit near a wall, next to the only other woman in the room. The dervishes were in everyday clothes, and they looked like friends gathered for a gossip session. In fact, they gossiped and laughed while the musicians arranged the instruments. Then the ney player put his lips to the ney and the music began.

> Listen to the tale of the reed's heart-felt
>   pain,
> For it tells the story of every separation:
> "Since they tore me from the reed-bed
>   where I belong
> "People have expressed their sorrow
>   through my song.
> "Whoever was left far from the land of his
>   origin,
> "Will surely seek reunion with her kin."

Rumi's masterpiece, the Mathnawi, begins with these lines, as translated by Fatemeh Keshavarz. The sorrow of the ney, the flute, is also what makes its music so sweet and haunting. This tension between longing and belonging is the lifeblood of the sema. It flowed now throughout the room in spiraling waves. The dervishes gathered in the circle slowly started swaying to the music and chanting the names of God. The word *Hu*, held tenderly and repeated with reverence, swooshed through the room. "What is Hu?" I once asked a Sufi teacher. Hu is the secret that everyone knows, she told me. Now it reverberated around the room, soft like a drone, fast like a gasp. We were all inside the sound, as if it were a ship at sea, rocking us gently.

One of the dervishes rose slowly, bowed, and started whirling in the middle of the circle. All the things I noticed about him first—his frayed sweater and corduroy pants, his old-man body with its paunchy middle—fell away as he turned on one foot while the other foot spun around and around and around. He was pure form now, a spiral of trembling concentration, climbing higher and higher. Then the slowing down. When he took his seat again, another dervish rose to whirl. And then another, filling that small ordinary space with the mystery of grace.

Once a month, an official sema performance takes place at the Konya Town Hall, an imposing white monolith on the outskirts of the city. In the beautiful central hall, Konya's Dervish Troupe offers a magnificently orchestrated sema. I had gathered with other tourists to watch that sema. If that sema was as grand as a rising sun, this one was as tender as the unfurling of a flower. There was nothing orchestrated about it; it was simply a few old men gathering to pray on a Thursday.

When it was over, my heart was beating loudly, but there was no sign that anything spiritually extraordinary had taken place in the room. Someone went to the kitchen to bring a platter of fruit and halwa. It was time for refreshments. Somebody else coughed and cleared his throat. Enis Abey turned to me and the other woman and gestured toward us to join the circle of men.

A man once chased me out of the Ninety-Sixth Street mosque in New York, the city's biggest mosque, because I had wandered into the main room, which was only for men. In Kozhikode in India, at one of the oldest mosques in the country, the imam shut the door in my face. In

Turkey, too, men's spaces and women's spaces were clearly separated in most mosques. However, in many of the grand Ottoman mosques in Istanbul, women's spaces were often artfully designed spaces built into the topography of the mosques. They were not afterthoughts or basements. In these Turkish mosques, I had started praying again, joining the congregation for communal prayers if I arrived in time or offering the brief movements of the "greeting the mosque" prayers. After years of musty corridors and screened-off corners, these spaces felt luxurious, and I began to understand what architecture can do for the spirit. I had arrived in these mosques as a tourist with a checklist of things to see, but the generosity of their soaring roofs and their soft carpets, offered freely to all who wanted to pray, reminded me how much I loved the fluidity between stillness and movement in namaz, the choir of ameens, the encounter of foreheads and floors. Turkish mosques spoiled me. I am no longer capable of praying in corridors and corners and basements while men monitor mosques like immigration officers. I don't want to be part of any mosque where women are treated like terrorists, our bodies like bombs waiting to go off. That night in Konya, when Enis Abey invited me to join the circle of men, it was perhaps the first time in my life that men in a mosque made me feel welcome.

Perhaps this welcome was offered so freely because I was a tourist. The other woman was a traveler from Syria. Perhaps we were invited into the circle because we were so clearly outside it. It is often easier for the traveling outsiders to transgress boundaries. But it is also true that Turkish Sufism has been a hospitable place for women.

As we ate fruit from the platter, I told Enis Abey about my plans to visit Meram.

"So you are going to visit Tavuz Khatun?" he said.

"You mean Tavuz Baba?"

"Hayir, hayir, Tavuz Khatun," he responded, nodding his head emphatically. The other dervishes started chiming in, correcting each other and throwing in colorful details. Here's the story I pieced together:

One day, the rebap music that would waft every day into Konya from the Meram hillside was not heard. The dervishes wondered what could have happened. The Mevlana sent some messengers to Meram to find out if Tavuz Baba was okay. The messengers looked everywhere in the house, but there was no one there. On the floor, however, were two peacock feathers. Then a villager from Meram told them this: the mysterious rebab player whom the dervishes never met, the fakir from India, was a woman who always dressed as a man. She did this for her safety. Traveling and living alone as she did, Tavuz Khatun's best protection was to disguise her beauty. But the villagers had known because one morning she had come out to feed the peacocks and her freshly washed, lustrous hair had given her away. They never knew when she died or how. The peacocks that she loved so much had carried her body away. The dervishes went back to Konya and told Rumi what had happened. Since then, Tavuz Khatun's house has been revered as a mosque.

The next day, I took a dolmus to Meram from Aladdin Caddesi. When we started out, we were packed as tightly as the dolmas from which the minibuses get their name. But as the landscape started turning rural, the crowds thinned out. The bus slowly emptied itself, and by the time I arrived at Meram, I was the last person to disembark. The driver pointed up the hill. There was nobody else to ask for directions, so I made my way up the hill toward a faraway cluster of buildings on the hillside. All I found there was a shuttered restaurant and pay toilets for men and women. Woods all around.

Just then I saw a man coming down the hill. "Turbesi nerede?" I asked him.

He turned around and gestured to me to follow him. A tall gaunt man, he seemed to have a kind face. I caught up with him. The path got narrow and isolated. The sun had set, and the winter evening was setting in way too fast for my comfort. Soon he was pushing brambles out of the way for us. I wondered if he, too, was lost. As we zigzagged through the woods, alarm bells started clanging inside my head. This was extremely strange behavior, and I knew I should stop following him. But if I stopped following him and he turned out to not be a rapist or murderer, how insulting would that be? My choices were terrible: either I would be raped and dismembered or I would offend him. How could I possibly choose between these two equally bad options?

Just then, we heard footsteps, and there were two men walking toward us through the woods. They were gesturing at us to stop. The stranger I was walking with turned to me.

"Turbesi? Ozür dilerim, I misunderstood. It is that way," he said, pointing toward a stone stairway that was cut into the hillside. Before I could thank him, he had walked away with long loping strides. I saw now that the stairway led to a mosque and next to it was the unmistakable green mound of a Sufi saint's tomb.

The other two men reached me. One of them was wearing a security guard's uniform and the other was a policeman.

"Persian?" the security guard asked me. He seemed agitated.

"Hayir, Hindistani," I replied.

"Madame, the man, the man"—he gestured to my side to indicate the man who had been walking by my side—"nerede?"

I shrugged and pointed backward.

"Madame," the security guard continued, trying to find English words. "He bad man, no good. Where he take you?"

In the conversation that followed, they told me the man was a local thug and having followed him into the woods was a very bad idea. Of course it was. Why had I trusted him so easily? How could my instincts have been so wrong? I felt the cold mountain breeze go up my spine. I had received so much generosity and hospitality in the last few days that I had started taking it for granted. The security guard at the restaurant had seen me follow him and had decided to check on me. They led me to the mosque amid a flow of anecdotes in Turkish that seemed to be all about the "bad man's" various misdeeds. Could one man in a small village have actually committed all these crimes? Now that I was surrounded by uniformed law and order, I felt brave enough to feel sorry for the "bad man." How had he acquired his reputation? Was it possible, perhaps, that he had merely lost his way? Maybe he was just the village misfit, doomed to be the "bad man." I would never know.

I visited Tavuz Khatun's tomb. I washed my hands, face, and feet in the chilly tap water in the courtyard. I could see the village that lay on the other side of the hill from the bus stop. Golden lights pricked the houses, and dinner smoke was rising from chimneys. A few schoolboys were sitting on the low wall of the mosque chattering. It was all so picturesque it reminded me of movies set in picturesque Turkish villages. I had gorged on so many while waiting for my visa to come through.

A few minutes later, the imam arrived and opened the mosque. He politely hid his puzzlement at my appearance and greeted me with his hand on his heart. The mosque was a simple two-room building in stone and wood. The sound of the azaan rang through the hills. I sat in the women's section, all by myself. The imam cleared his throat and started praying. Cut off by a wall between us, I listened to his cues. We were praying together and we were praying alone. We were a congregation moving together on either side of the wall that separated us. Standing in front of God. Fatiha, the opening of the Qur'an. Bowing from the waist. The prostration, the feel of the floor on my forehead. Salaams to the malak on the right and the malak on the left. I have always believed in these malaks. Never seen them, never heard them, but every day I have felt their breath on

me, like the prayers of my ancestors, the dreams of the people who inhabited before me the houses I lived in, the bene-
dictions of the writers I have loved.

As I crossed my legs under me on the borrowed prayer
rug, I felt the flutter of my own presence, my aliveness, my
being there in that moment. I prayed for my family, waiting
for me in India. I prayed for the people of Konya who had
offered me hospitality and made room for me in their lives.
I prayed for myself, to find love and faith. Is loneliness a way
of feeling deeply present, of feeling the weight of the choices
that have brought you to a particular moment, a particular place? As the twilight hour came to sit lightly on the
Meram mountains, I savored my loneliness. Like praying
alone, traveling alone too is a dance between solitude and
loneliness. You are a congregation of one. You feel the absence of others praying with you, around you, behind you.
Because without that absence, how would you know the
sweetness of sharing your most intimate soliloquies with
the Presence?

I stepped out of the mosque and turned toward the
green tomb for one more look. So many centuries ago, he/
she/they must have arrived here, crossing rivers and deserts, bending genders, squaring curves, befriending peacocks because humans could not be trusted. I thought of
all the young women who travel—the intrepid ones and the
shy ones—against all the odds piled up on our way. How
strong and curious we are. How hungrily we had fallen on
travel and guidebooks and the world itself as it opened up

to us. How vulnerable we are, in ways that most men rarely are. There must be malaks looking out for us, wishing us peace from either side, thrilling with pride when we reach our destinations and grieving with peacocks when we don't.

Chapter

TWO

✈

THE FIRST TIME I LOST MY PASSPORT WAS IN JAPAN. I WAS eighteen years old, and we were in the airport in Kyoto. Krishna, another Indian teen, and I were the winners of a debate contest organized by a Japanese organization, and this trip—two weeks of traveling around Japan—was our prize. From Kyoto we were to go to Hiroshima. When we got to the gate of our flight and were asked to present our passports, mine was nowhere to be found.

I was not at all worried. My brand-new Indian passport had arrived only a few weeks before my trip to Japan, and to me it was just a booklet. Our guide, Tanaka-San, a kindly businessman who had been saddled with the burden of chaperoning us around Japan, looked extremely unhappy, but by now Krishna and I had pegged him as a worrier. In the mornings, we were frequently late to meet him in our hotel lobby, and it was clear even this small misdemeanor was too much for Tanaka-San. Steeped in Indian Stretchable Time as we were, Krishna and I were clueless about how thoughtless we were. So when I could not find my passport and Tanaka-San looked unhappy, I didn't give it much thought. I was an adolescent; I was practiced at losing things. It would turn up eventually, I thought, or we would find a way around the problem.

In a few minutes, the passport was found in a restroom in between security and the flight gate. A young man with a serious smile brought it to the lounge and left with a little bow. I had left it on the counter of the restroom sink. Someone had rescued it and handed it in to the airport authorities. A few drops of water had spilled on it, but it was not much worse for the wear. We boarded our flights.

Now I always know where my passport is. Right now, it is in the drawer of the secretary desk in my living room in New York, the one with the broken lid carefully propped up. The drawer also has our vaccination cards, our Overseas Citizen of India cards, and a random assortment of various currencies, waiting to be in circulation again. If you are an immigrant, you, too, probably have one of these drawers. The Document Drawer and the Spice Box—these are the poles that mark the axis around which my immigrant household spins.

One night a few years ago, when we were sleeping, I woke up to the smell of smoke. The building next door was on fire. It was March 2020, and schools and workplaces had just begun shutting down. The pandemic was still in the don't-wear-a-mask stage of public information. We ran out of the apartment, quickly grabbing wallets. As we gathered on the street outside, watching firefighters hose down flames next door and rescue the building's residents and hoping that the flames would not spread, I thought of our passports—sitting safely in the Document Drawer upstairs. It was then that the panic that should have struck me years ago in Kyoto truly struck. I imagined my newly acquired U.S. passport going up in flames, in the middle of a pandemic, while we were all at the mercy of an administration that had already delayed naturalization procedures.

Again I was lucky. The firefighters contained the flames and, eventually, we all went upstairs. And in fact, if my passport had indeed been eaten by the fire, I would probably have been just fine reapplying for a replacement passport. I didn't know this in March 2020, but that passport was going nowhere for a few years. On the other hand, if I had truly lost my passport in Kyoto, I would have faced much more trouble as a tourist with a return flight to catch in a few days.

Yet, between that first international trip and now, my relationship with my passport has become so much more fraught. It's not just that I grew up. The world is a different place. Traveling blithely through Japan in 1997, I had to explain again and again that I was not Hindu, that Islam was not a version of Hinduism. For some reason, everyone seems to have heard of Islam and Muslims since then. And of course I am no longer a teenager with a casual attitude to Things. I am an Extremely Responsible Adult and I never have to ask my child to find my glasses. I no longer leave my passport in airport restrooms.

But there are other ways to lose a passport. Between the bathroom sink in Kyoto and the neighborhood fire in Brooklyn, I lost my Indian passport forever. One day a couple of years before the fire, I winced my way through the Oath of Allegiance at a naturalization ceremony at the

Brooklyn Borough Hall and acquired a U.S. passport. That put me in the strange situation of applying for a visa to go home to India. The Indian government required a certificate of renunciation of my Indian passport before I could apply for a visa. So a few weeks after pledging allegiance to one nation, I walked into an office in midtown Manhattan to renounce my allegiance to another.

It is a pretty harsh word, isn't it, *renunciation*. I had never renounced anything until then, though I had heard of saints renouncing the world or kings renouncing thrones. In a process filled with forms and prepaid labels and passport-size photos, the word *renunciation* offered a glimmer of the melodrama of the moment. It made my Indian passport feel like the throne to a kingdom.

The story of my renunciation began long before, in 2010. It was a beautiful fall day in New York, and my husband, Rollo, said: "Imagine that you have a rich millionaire boyfriend and he is whisking you off to Paris for a long weekend." We were sitting on the beat-up couch we got for free from a neighbor. I was four months pregnant, and we were considering doing something special before the baby arrived and changed our lives forever.

When Rollo was twenty-one, he spent two months in Paris doing nothing. Every evening, he ate at a restaurant where the chef cooked whatever she wanted and guests played the guitar in the corner. He didn't go to a single museum. He always says *Paris* as if the word were a demitasse of coffee and he was stirring sugar into it.

I, on the other hand, had never been to Paris.

Well, that's not true.

I once had to transit through Paris after Royal Jordanian rerouted me after overbooking my flight from Mumbai to New York. So I arrived in Paris in the middle of the night without a "transit visa," which I did not know I needed. I spent most of the night in a small, windowless corridor of a room, with about a dozen other brown and Black people whose passports disqualified us from walking through the airport freely. When I went to the bathroom, a police officer kicked the door open after a few minutes. He did not apologize.

Early the next day, the airport police asked me to sign a statement. When I asked for a translator, the police officer who was questioning me turned fuchsia in the face and yelled at me. Finally, a young Asian woman came to translate, and she translated with so much sympathy that I burst into all the tears I had held back until then. She told me not to worry, that Immigration was having me escorted to the other airport in the company of two police officers and that the statement I was signing was to acknowledge that the police escort was of my own volition, not an arrest. I signed.

My first view of Paris was from the window of the police car that took me from the Charles de Gaulle Airport to the Orly Airport.

So *Paris*, the word, always makes my shoulders brace. A face floats into my mind: the North African man who sat opposite me in the detention corridor that night in Paris. He was there before I arrived and he was there when I left.

When a policeman called out my name so I could go get interrogated, he looked at me and nodded with a kind of bored despair. Whenever someone mentions Paris, I think of him and wonder how long he sat in the corridor waiting for his name to be called.

And yet I was tempted by this other Paris, the romance capital. What would it be like to walk through that city and not think of the city of windowless airport-interrogation rooms? Since my unfortunate Paris layover, I had been to other parts of France, always skirting Paris. But suddenly it seemed silly to let one bad experience put me off forever. And what would it be like to enjoy Paris as a tourist, armed with the reflected glow of my husband's white American privilege? After all, who was I to resist Paris? Could you even say you had traveled if you had never been to Paris?

Paris is often called the most visited city in the world. It's as if there is a Paris-shaped lacuna in the life of every tourist until they visit the city. A couple of million Americans visit Paris every year. Interestingly, the average American would not have thought of France as a tourism destination until well into the twentieth century. Prior to that, European travel from the United States was largely limited to the wealthy, soldiers, businesspeople, and diplomats. It was the twentieth century that made Paris an American destination, beginning with U.S. troops who carried back Paris's reputation as a city of pleasures. In the flurry of postwar travels, many American writers and artists made themselves at home in Paris. *A Moveable Feast* and *Tender Is the Night* and *The Autobiography of Alice B. Toklas* captured the life of these expatriate American bohemians in the Left Bank. It was the beginning of an enduring American Francophilia.

This turned out to be an extremely convenient infatuation after the Second World War, when France was in ruin after the German invasion. In *We'll Always Have Paris: American Tourists in France since 1930*, Harvey Levenstein writes of how the Marshall Plan spurred the revival of tourism in postwar France. The multibillion-dollar five-year American-aid program was aimed at rebuilding the western European countries as a bulwark against Soviet Communism and as a market for American goods. France, whose powerful Communist Party lurked at the threshold of power, was the centerpiece of this effort.

In early 1948, three thousand Americans descended on Paris to run the Marshall Plan. At nearly the same time, a host of CIA operatives and government public relations officers arrived in Paris (Paul Cushing Child, Julia Child's husband, among them). The city was flooded with thousands of Americans, most of them recruited from elite Ivy League universities, which were, as Levenstein notes, part of "the same circles where traveling to France was much appreciated." Monte Carlo sent croupiers over to the United States to learn how to run craps tables the way Americans did. Norman Mailer wrote in disgust to a friend, "All the fucking Americans are here."

They were not, of course. And nobody realized this better than French tourism officials who set their eyes on, as the commissioner of tourism Henri Legrande put it, "the great middle-class from America, which has not traveled to foreign countries." Marshall Plan officials enthusiastically supported the French campaign for middle-class American tourism. That was a better use of Plan dollars than reviving the inefficient French industry. It would also mean that French manufacturing would not be competing with American manufacturing. In a triple win, dollars earned from tourism could then be used to buy American-made goods.

And so, developing tourism to France became an important objective of the Marshall Plan. In *Overbooked*, Elizabeth Becker writes of how French hoteliers and restaurateurs were sent to the United States for training in American consumer tastes: plump pillows, bedside lamps for reading, hotel gift shops. An especially astute calculation was to market Paris as a convention venue. The French government convinced officials at the Marshall Plan to underwrite more hotel rooms and large meeting rooms to encourage well-populated American associations to hold their conferences in Paris. And to top it all off, the Plan spent millions on advertisements to convince Americans to travel to France.

Working together, the Marshall Plan and French tourism officials eliminated the shortage of steamships on the North Atlantic, encouraged off-season tourism, organized low-cost tours, and cut the red tape at border crossings. The French government was only too happy to cooperate. For instance, despite continuing electricity shortages, the government arranged for the great sites of Paris such as Notre Dame and Place de la Concorde to be flooded with light at night. "Fall is fine in France," they advertised to older Americans who were able to make off-season visits. The Plan's plan worked all too well. In 1951, *An American in Paris*, a film about a former G.I. who decided to remain in Paris after the war to pursue his lifelong dream of becoming a painter, won the Academy Award for best picture. The rest of Europe fell quickly. "But if it's Tuesday, it has to be Siena," a confused American tourist tells another as they are about to board a tour bus somewhere in Europe, in a 1957 *New Yorker* cartoon. By 1969, there was a movie, *If It's Tuesday, This Must Be Belgium*. France served as the gateway drug for the rest of Europe.

Even today, for so many Americans, France has the quality of a sweet dream. Moving to France, learning French, mastering the art of French cooking, adopting French women's beauty and diet tips, raising children as the French do: perhaps no other national group harbors as many French fantasies as Americans. The American wanderlust for France has a solid but invisible bedrock in the infrastructure and advertising that was sponsored by the Marshall Plan more than seven decades ago. So often, the middle-class wanderlust that is responsible for the mass tourism that we all participate in has the same recipe: infrastructure and advertising, the government and the private sector, working together to create smoothly oiled machinery that throws dream-sparks into our consciousness: "Disneyland!" "Taj Mahal!" "Imagine! Your rich millionaire boyfriend is taking you to Paris!"

"Only if you can keep our round-trip tickets under a thousand dollars," I said from the couch as Rollo hunted for fares. "Done!" he said. "Only a little more than a thousand." Before I could ask the details, he added, "Don't worry, I'll do all the work for your visa application."

With his American passport, Rollo did not need a visa; he could simply walk into France. With my Indian passport, not only did I need to apply for a visa, but I also had to interview in person at a French consulate and pay a visa-application fee.

It would be too vague to call this discrimination racism. The scholar Srđan Mladenov Jovanović writes about the importance of a separate term that differentiates citizenship-based discrimination from racism and xenophobia. We know that the inequality of passportism has been baked into immigration policy. But tourism has also played a big part in normalizing it. Jovanović writes, "Passportism can thus be broadly defined as the speech, policy or act of a discriminative nature, in which an individual or a group of individuals are discriminated against on the basis of their citizenship, i.e. passport." While racism discriminates on the basis of the color of a person's skin, passportism discriminates on the basis of the color of a person's passport. Passportism is the fear of Third World passports. And while there has been some recent, much-needed reckoning among travel publications about how racism impacts travel, there has been no such reckoning about passportism and its big and small humiliations.

Passportism can strike at unexpected moments. In 1999, the year after he won the Nobel Prize in Economics, Amartya Sen was on his way to speak at the World Economic Forum in Davos. After his flight landed at Zurich airport, he was detained and questioned by its airport police because he was an Indian passport holder without a visa. "The police were very skeptical about my financial means," Sen recalled later in an interview with *The New York Times*. Not satisfied with his U.S. residency card or the letter from the Swiss authorities promising him a visa at the Davos airport, they asked him to produce a bank statement. Only after he convinced them that he was solvent and would not become a burden on the Swiss state was Amartya Sen allowed to enter Switzerland and deliver his speech titled "Responsible Globality: Managing the Impact of Globalization."

The "transit visa" is one of passportism's slyest tools. In an eloquent essay titled "The Color of Our Passports," Tabish Khair, an Indian writer based in Denmark, writes about the perils of not giving up his Indian passport. Khair recalls trying to board a flight from Copenhagen to an academic conference in Munich, armed with his ticket, his Indian passport, his Danish permanent visa, and the letters from his employers in Denmark as well as the conference organizers in Munich—if this seems excessive to you, you have never had a Third World passport. This is how we travel.

But Khair's connecting flight was through London, and someone had changed the rules a few days prior to his flight. It used to be that transit visas were required only if you had to leave the London airport, but now he was politely informed at the airport in Copenhagen, people with certain kinds of passports needed a transit visa simply to get out of one plane and board another in London. "The colour of my passport was wrong," Khair writes.

What exactly, I sometimes wonder, do immigration

officials think will happen in the usually hectic hours that we have to transit from one airport to another airport or from one plane to another plane? It is as if we are novice monks who must wear transit-visa chastity belts lest the brief glimpse of Paris or London suddenly unbuckle any commitment we have to our current lives. The annals of Third World travelers are full of stories like these, and they are minor humiliations compared to the trauma and uncertainty that mark the lives of many refugees and immigrants. But the passportism that lies under this wide range of pain is based on the same power hierarchy.

Unlike many other forms of discrimination, it is a hierarchy that can be mathematically ranked, on the basis of the access provided to other countries and the time spent in applying and going through the visa process. The Covid-19 pandemic initially wreaked havoc on passport hierarchies—in April 2020, the U.S. passport fell dramatically in the ranking, but as vaccination rates entrenched the rich-poor gaps between countries, it recovered. On the other hand, South Korea and the United Arab Emirates have been steadily climbing the passport index—a sure sign of shifting geopolitical realities.

Even as the Indian passport encounters passportism outside its borders, the Indian immigration authorities practice passportism toward citizens of countries they deem unfriendly or dangerous. Visitors from many African countries and most Muslim countries, as well as those who can trace their heritage to Pakistan, routinely find their visa applications rejected, especially as the right-wing government

that has been in power since 2014 grinds down civil liberties. Thus the passportism hierarchy is not just a simple
East-West binary; it is more akin to a caste system with
multiple strata, clearly marked in a descending order. Many
Third World countries including India have internalized
passportism. In Africa, despite the African Union's attempt
to launch a continent-wide common passport, many of the
richer countries make it harder for fellow Africans to visit
them as compared to European visitors. This is particularly
ironic given that many of Africa's borders are arbitrary lines
drawn on a map of the continent during the Berlin Conference of 1884, in which the continent was carved up among
the colonial powers.

Passportism has also opened up new avenues in global
real estate and finance. Take, for instance, Arton Capital,
which maintains the Arton Passport Index: "the only real-
time global ranking of the world's passports, updated as frequently as new visa waivers and changes are implemented."
Arton Capital focuses on "impact investment programs
for residence and citizenship"; in other words, they help
wealthy people in Third World countries figure out how to
acquire First World passports through real estate and other
financial investments. At the most obvious level, Arton
Capital seems to be an immigration agency for HNWIs—
people who are so wealthy that in the time it takes to write
out *high-net-worth individuals*, they could have made a few
million.

But beneath that somewhat benign disguise is an active financial channel that connects expensive investment

projects in First World countries with eager Third World investors. Golden visas and economic citizenship programs are an easy source of cash for countries that have strong passports. In return, the country gains a particularly obedient set of investors—their goal is not so much to make profit as it is to buy their way into a richer country. Arton calls this a "global citizenship movement." It is in the interest of assisting its investors to make the most up-to-date decisions that Arton Capital maintains a passport index.

In much the same way that, in the United States, parents of school-age children will try to rent or buy homes in zip codes with "good school districts," billionaire migrants can now shop around the globe for real estate that will enable their access to the best educational and lifestyle prospects. Australia, the United States, and Canada all have lucrative programs that trade passports or permanent visas for investment, targeting wealthy migrants fleeing China, Brazil, India, and Turkey. Debt-laden European countries, such as Portugal, Spain, and Greece, offer an alternative to those who would prefer their economic citizenship with a discount. In fact, according to Andrew Henderson, who runs the website Nomad Capitalist, the pandemic was a time of fire sale for the "immigration investment industry," with several countries lowering their prices or even launching special deals. Thus, passportism has helped create side hustles for the countries that benefit from being at the top of the passport hierarchy.

But in 2011, lying on our thirdhand couch listening to French-language lessons while my husband assembled my

French visa application—we didn't know all this. We were almost a decade away from the pandemic. Travel still felt like a disproportionately pleasurable recreational activity. Or maybe it was that we didn't have a child yet. We had Time and Energy. Surely a little French passportism could not stop us.

•

"France is well in the way of passportism," says the fifth volume of Chambers's Pocket Miscellany, a series of essay collections edited by William and Robert Chambers, Edinburgh-based publishers, starting in 1829. This is the earliest reference to passportism I've found, and the author is describing how annoying it is to be asked for a passport when he travels outside Britain. In resentful detail, he outlines the suffering of a British man who is detained by a sentinel for smoking a cigar in Prussia and has to spend the night in the guardhouse.

These words were published in the middle of the nineteenth century, the dawn of modern tourism. It had only been a couple of decades since trains had become a form of public transportation, nine years after the first Thomas Cook expedition. According to Martin Lloyd in *The Passport: The History of Man's Most Travelled Document*, for the upper-class British traveler of this era, a passport was a tiresome document. So many countries did not require it, which made it especially annoying that France did.

It seems remarkable from my perspective in the first

quarter of the twenty-first century that there was a time
when many people traveled abroad without passports. But
in the nineteenth century, travelers from wealthy countries such as the United States and the United Kingdom
frequently moved through the world undocumented, fully
confident that their bearing and social class made a passport unnecessary. Passport officials had a great degree of
discretion in choosing to ask to see a passport or not. Across
the Atlantic, Lloyd notes, the constitutions of Mexico and
many South American countries, including Venezuela,
Uruguay, Ecuador, Bolivia, and Peru, provided the right
to travel freely without a passport to all foreigners. Many
guidebooks of the time indicate that while passports were
not needed for travel, they could be useful for reclaiming
packages at the post office or changing money.

When it did exist, the nineteenth-century passport
was usually a single sheet of paper, tucked into a traveler's
wallet. A single passport could apply to an entire group of
travelers, including servants. Sometimes, it described the
passport holder; often it did not. Photos were not required
until the twentieth century after a German spy imperson-
ated an American during the First World War. The passport
frequently functioned as a kind of entry permit, more akin
to the modern visa, rather than a document of nationality.
Passports were issued by a person's country of nationality
but also by other countries—if you lost your passport while
traveling abroad (or if you were British and had simply not
bothered to get one), you could apply for a passport from
the country in which you found yourself. They could be

issued by Italian duchies, German kingdoms, and mayors in the United States. They were hardly passports as we think of them today.

Prior to the nineteenth century, passports were much more commonly used as domestic documents. A commoner in eighteenth-century France had to have either a passport issued by the local town hall or an "aveu," a character certificate from the local church. The point was to make it difficult for peasants to migrate to cities, especially Paris. Elsewhere in Europe, internal passports were used to control the movements of "gypsies" and "vagabonds." At the turn of the eighteenth century, Lloyd writes, the lowliest Continental agricultural worker who wanted to walk thirty miles down the road had to possess a passport describing him down to the color of his eyebrows and the shape of his chin. (The much-hated passport system was briefly overthrown in the immediate wake of the French Revolution but was quickly reinstated after it was found useful in preventing the French aristocracy from emigrating to friendly countries with their baubles.) And while the upper-class British were affronted by having to acquire passports for travel abroad, a 1662 law in England, adopted by Charles II, empowered the local authorities to remove to their place of legal settlement anyone likely to become a public charge.

I have often used the word *passport* as a metaphor for mobility. But the more I read passport history, the more I realize that preventing mobility is the real ancestry of the modern passport. While it is tempting to look on passports as documents of access, enabling us to move freely through the world, they are, in fact, documents that started out preventing travel, or permitting travel only along state-approved itineraries.

The passport's ancient origins hint at this state control of private movement. The Old Testament records that the prophet Nehemiah required letters from King Artaxerxes (of modern-day Iraq) to the governors of lands across the Euphrates so he could travel freely through them when he went to Palestine. Roman emperors are known to have issued tractoriums to permit their officials to travel throughout the far reaches of the Roman Empire, and, according to the *Codex Theodosianus*, students who wanted to come to Rome had to first get permission documents from the judges in their local provinces. Passports have also been traced back to the safe-conduct documents issued by medieval kings to soldiers and negotiators of enemy countries.

Thus, right from the beginning, the power of a passport to facilitate travel is a corollary to the power of the state to deny passports and prevent travel. It was in modern times, however, that the passport as a state tool came into its own. John Torpey writes in *The Invention of Passport: Surveillance, Citizenship and the State* of how the rise of the modern nation-state is intertwined with its control of mobility. The "stateness" of a state, Torpey writes, stems from its ability to control who travels within and into its borders. The modern nation-state inherited this legacy from medieval kingdoms that zealously monitored the movement of the poor and marginalized.

In 1885, Canada introduced a "pass system" to control the movement of First Nations people. Without a pass, a First Nations person who was found outside their reserve could be incarcerated. Enslaved people in the American South were also required to carry a pass from their owners whenever they traveled beyond the borders of their owners' properties. In fact, during the Civil War, this domestic passport system was extended to whites as well, as various cities declared martial law and prepared for a federal invasion, thus leading to the ironic sight of white and Black people waiting in the same passport offices. This is one of the central ironies of the passport system. The same passport that represented mobility to one set of people represented restrictions to another group, in the same way that a First World passport today opens doors that a Third World passport can only dream of from a distance.

These internal passports are rarely remembered when we talk of passport history, but the systems of surveillance and control they built are the bedrock on which the modern passport rests much more comfortably and glamorously. The nineteenth-century French passport system was extended to control the mobility of foreign travelers. A traveler arriving in a French port had to surrender their passport, which was forwarded to Paris and had to be retrieved in person from the prefecture of police. Hotel concierges had to submit foreign passports to the local police station for a second checking. Today, these obsessive-compulsive rituals have been written into the law in many countries in Europe as well as in Asia, causing hotels to keep extensive passport records for the use of governments—and whoever can hack into hotel reservation systems. In 2018, Marriott Hotels discovered a four-year-long data breach in its system, as a result of which 339 million guest records were exposed to Chinese government-sponsored hackers. Still, we are told, this is for our own security.

Why is it that our passports today are modeled on that old French system? In 1782, after the United States won its own war of independence, close on the heels of the French Revolution, the new nation's first-ever diplomat, Benjamin Franklin, who was a Francophile, modeled the text of the American passport on the French version. The rise of tourism and the vagaries in which nineteenth-century British tourists, traveling abroad in much larger numbers than those of any other country, found themselves on the Continent prompted the British Parliament to take a leaf from the French. Colonization helped make the French passport even more widespread. As Martin Lloyd writes, the passport system as practiced in nineteenth century Europe was not the only system in the world that involved tokens of permission and identity, but it became the most widespread simply through European imperialism. Europeans brought their administrative systems to Africa, Asia, and the Americas. And so, a system primarily created to control the movements of peasants to Paris became the basis for power and permission in international travel around the world.

·

In 2010, with my Indian passport, this is what I needed for the French visa application:

> a valid passport
> ID photograph
> proof of my legal status in the U.S.A.
> document describing the planned program
> (letter of invitation; reservation
> confirmation of an organized trip)
> prebooked round-trip ticket
> travel health insurance certificate
> proof of accommodation
> copies of bank statements for the last three
> months
> letter from my employer
> application fee of sixty euros

This is what my husband needed for his application: nothing. He did not need a visa at all. He could simply walk into France, straight off the airplane.

Every place we had traveled to together until then, from Cambodia to Slovenia, my husband, with his U.S. passport, had walked straight off the airplane into the foreign country, while I waited in a line to be seen by immigration. In reparation, my husband had offered to do all the paperwork for every visa application or immigration document.

This meant that before he could start on my France visa application, he had to check the status of my Advance Parole online. We had just applied for my green card—the little card that would change my status from nonresident alien to permanent resident. The Advance Parole was the document that would let me travel back to the United States while the green card was being processed. We could not apply for a French visa till we had the Advance Parole. It was a nesting doll of paperwork. We were trapped in a video game with higher and higher levels of form-filling.

And yet we were enormously privileged in that all my documents were in order and I was not a risk to the U.S. government in terms of health, criminal record, public charge, or security. With help from my husband's white privilege and the expertise of an immigration lawyer, I had cleared one hurdle after another. Now we waited for the Advance Parole. "Any day now." That's what our immigration lawyer told us when we asked him when it would arrive.

"The website says it is pending," my husband reported before turning back to assemble my France visa application. He grabbed a folder and made a list. He was humming to himself cheerfully as he began to gather copies of my pay stubs. The humming stopped when he got to the bank statements. By the time he started collecting my income tax returns, the mood was definitely grim. But it was the passport photo that finally did him in. Per the website of the consulate of France, the photo needed to show my hairline and my ears. Drawers were pulled out; files were shaken. But in every single passport photo in our possession, my hair was covering my ears. "This is so fucking stupid." My husband threw up his hands. "Why why why?"

•

The colorful history of the Western passport does not account entirely for passportism against Third World countries. For the crucial piece of subtext missing in this history, we have to read between the lines. In the nineteenth century, the British had made it a common practice to move around indentured labor between their colonies. However, when its colonized people started using their status as Commonwealth subjects to move around of their own free will, the British government realized the dangers posed by this open-door policy. In her brilliant book *Indian Migration and Empire: A Colonial Genealogy of the Modern State*, Radhika Mongia writes about how the migration of about two thousand Sikh men to Canada in 1905 prompted a long chain of pearl-clutching correspondence. The men had "doubtless come under misrepresentation as they are not suited to the climate, and there is not sufficient field for their employment. Many are in danger of becoming public charge and are subject to deportation under the law of Canada," the governor general of Canada telegrammed to the secretary of state for the colonies in London. This concern trolling would prove to be unfounded: by 1907, all but fifty to sixty of the men had found employment. It's also safe to assume that they managed to find appropriate winter clothing and kept themselves warm.

But as Mongia notes, this unprecedented migration created an interesting administrative conundrum for the empire upon which the sun was not supposed to set: "how to distinguish between British subjects, members of a single expansionist state, without calling the entire edifice of the empire into question." How does one prevent colonized people from moving freely through the colonies without striking an obviously racist-colonial stance?

Working together, the governor general of Canada (whose goal was to safeguard Canada's whiteness), the secretary of state for the colonies in London (whose goal was to keep the empire strong), and the British government in India (whose goal was to pretend that Indian colonialism was a force of good) came up with an elaborate scheme that involved, among other rules, a policy that only travelers on continuous journeys from their port of origin would be allowed to enter Canada. Since there were no shipping companies plying nonstop between India and Vancouver, this effectively halted immigration from India.

Problem solved until 1914. On May 23, 1914, the *Komagata Maru* arrived off the coast of Vancouver carrying 376 passengers, mostly Sikhs. Hired by Sardar Gurdit Singh, an Indian entrepreneur with sympathies to the Ghadar movement (a diasporic political movement to overthrow British rule in India), the *Komagata Maru* had artfully managed to fulfill the continuous-journey requirement by having its Indian passengers board the ship in Hong Kong and Shanghai and Yokohama, from the Indian diasporas located there.

All the storms that the *Komagata Maru* encountered on the high seas could not have prepared it for the storm of racist outrage unleashed against it as it sat for two months in the Vancouver harbor. Not only were the passengers not allowed to disembark; a military launch patrolled the ship constantly to ensure that it could not even dock. The local South Asian community advocated fiercely for the ship's passengers and raised money to keep paying the charter fees that became due since the ship did not return to its owners. But they were not allowed to help the passengers, who rapidly ran out of food and sat half a mile from the Canadian shore, starving and harassed, while the former prime minister, Wilfrid Laurier, now in the opposition, declared in the Canadian Parliament: "The people of Canada want to have a white country."

After two months, the *Komagata Maru* was forced to sail back to India. It was escorted out of the Vancouver harbor by the Canadian Navy, prepared to shoot, and it was met in Calcutta by the British army, who declared the ship full of insurgents and shot and killed twenty passengers.

The *Komagata Maru* incident had revealed the hollowness of the continuous-journey regulation, and once again the question remained. How to prevent brown people, armed with the juridical definition of themselves as equal subjects of a huge empire, from moving into white countries? The problem was that the colonial government in India could not be seen to be obviously racist. There was a difference between shooting at "insurgents" and denying migration outright on the basis of skin color. So much had been invested in the propaganda of the British as just rulers, bringing fairness and equality to the tropics. Besides, the anticolonial movement in India was gathering strength, and the last thing the colonial government wanted to do was feed that fire.

The solution reached was to establish a passport system for Indians. This British Indian passport would entitle a traveler to admission anywhere in the colonies. But the number of these permits or passports would be limited. And it became a criminal offense to embark on a journey from any port in British India without a passport.

This is the useful paradox of the passport as a form of control. The passport would entitle, but the limited number of passports would disentitle. In one stroke, the seeming granting of a privilege would actually be the mechanism that took away a privilege that was freely available, at least theoretically, until then.

Luckily, the First World War was underway, and passport regulation was easily established under the aegis of security theater. The rules requiring passports from all Indians traveling outside India appear as the Defense of India (Passport) Rules. But, as Radhika Mongia points out, these were actually the Defense of a White Canada Rules. Not only did the passport allow the empire to absolve itself of racial motivations; it also permitted the exploitation of "security" as a potential realm for controlling the audacity of migration, and it consolidated the power of the empire as the sovereign authority that gets to decide who gets to travel. A passport is a pretty convenient thing to have—if you are a state.

The anxieties and suspicions of the First World War led more and more countries to institutionalize passports. It soon became clear that the document needed to be standardized across national systems. Starting in 1920, the newly formed League of Nations held a series of meetings that they called the International Conference on Passports, Customs Formalities and Through Tickets. Over the course of the interwar period, the thirty-two-page booklet-style "international passport," with the name of the issuing country on the cover and the first four pages devoted to the bearer's identity, as proposed by the conference, became more and more universal. Even the U.S.A., not a member of the League, introduced a passport in 1926 that followed most of the specifications laid down by the conference.

Periodically, the Conference, as well as others like it, would consider abolishing the passport, but with vast numbers of war refugees created after the world war, most European countries were reluctant to sign on to this. With the explosion of tourism after the Second World War and improvements in aviation that translated into increased movement possibilities—whether for migration or tourism—the dream of a passport-free world disappeared forever.

But again, within this seeming universalization, there emerged new hierarchies. As passports increasingly got standardized, visa controls also became more normalized. Travel-visa regulations became a useful extraterritorial policy tool to not only control immigration but also express geopolitical clout. Today, visas have become the primary method of controlling mobility. Visa-based restrictions enable states to preselect travelers of the right kind and deter would-be migrants. In a tweet, Josef Burton, a former U.S.

diplomat who worked in Turkey and India, described the U.S. visa officer as "an unquestionable black box capable of irreversible decisions they don't need to explain." Through the visa-granting and visa-denying power of consulates, the modern nation-state is able to extend its powers beyond its own borders.

It is a fundamental paradox of visa regimes that the poorer your nation is, the more you have to pay to obtain a visa, while the citizens of wealthy nations pay less or nothing at all. There is an injustice here at the level of human rights, but it is even more stark when we consider how free trade is thrust down the throats of poor countries, while free movement is so blithely denied. The paradox deepens when you adjust visa costs against the purchasing power of different currency regimes and the wage discrepancies across the globe. How does the cost of an average tourist visa translate across the world? An April 2021 article analyzed data sets of visa-application costs across the globe and concluded that while Western, Northern, and Southern Europeans, North Americans, and Australians and New Zealanders have to work for less than two hours to pay for the average tourist visa, Central Asians have to work more than ten days, Southern Asians have to work two weeks, and sub-Saharan Africans have to work three weeks to pay for the same document. Travel is not just less bureaucratic; it is also much cheaper with a Western passport. I shudder to think of all the money I have spent on visas and immigration. The application fees. The processing fees. The lawyer fees.

•

Suddenly our emails to the immigration lawyer didn't seem to be getting through. But after several follow-ups, he replied that we could try to expedite the process by submitting a letter stating that there was a family medical emergency abroad. If we got a letter from a doctor in India saying that one of my parents was dying and this was my last opportunity to see them, the system might be tricked into coughing up my Advance Parole a few days early.

I guess it was our fault. We did ask for *any* other ideas.

"I mean, maybe you should," joked a friend of mine to whom I reported this ridiculousness. Her parents had moved to the United States from the same part of Kerala where my father grew up. "Indian parents would prefer to die than have you lose a thousand dollars."

I will admit, it was the thought of losing those thousand dollars that gnawed at me the most. The flights we had already bought, with money rescued from the jaws of student loans and Brooklyn rents only to be thrown into the jowls of the airline industry. I had heard that babies were expensive. And there we were, gambling on visas and tickets instead of saving for a bigger apartment. Or a new laptop. Or a decent mattress to replace our ancient Ikea futon.

"Let's just think of it as dummy tax," Rollo said. This too was a gulf between us, the way we thought of money. From the earliest days of our relationship, we fell into these roles: the Spender and the Saver. What mattered more to him was that we might not go to Paris. Fall evenings on the Seine, bookstores on winding streets, cafés au lait, all that romantic crap. "If we don't go now, we might never go," he added after a minute. I knew what he meant. The opposite of "We'll always have Paris." I felt our studio apartment closing in around us. It was as if the arrival of a baby would mark the end of something carefree and spontaneous about our current lives. *Parents; we'll be parents*, I thought. *Parents don't go to Paris. Lovers do.*

Pending. This was what the website said every time we checked on my immigration status online. Our flight to Paris was only a couple of weeks away, and the Advance Parole still had not arrived. We checked again and again. *Maybe the website has not been updated*, we told ourselves as we checked the mail twice a day. The possibility of Paris was now trapped between two government documents: the Advance Parole from the U.S. government and the French visa.

Amid all this, a thought kept running at the back of my mind: *If only he had listened to me.* Perhaps every partner in every relationship has said words to this effect at one time or another. But it seemed to me also a reflection of a fundamental gulf between our experiences. Surely only a white American man would assume that if you take care of your paperwork in time, life will sort itself out. The rest of us know that immigration statuses and travel plans can never be taken for granted. The rest of us have stood in lines and tried to persuade stone-faced bureaucrats. The rest of us expect things to not go well.

•

One morning in my obstetrician's waiting room, I heard a woman sobbing. The sobs were coming through the thin walls behind me. All of us pregnant women leafing through magazines or eyeing the reality show on the TV slowly became alert. We did not dare to meet each other's eyes. A nurse hurried to the cubicle. "What is wrong, sweetie?"

"My baby died," the woman crying replied. A collective spasm of horror passed through the waiting room. Our hands shook; our lips trembled. Her sobs continued. Each one of us felt her grief, albeit in a diluted form that was accompanied by the selfish thought *Thank god thank god thank god that is not me.*

In the spectrum of human troubles, worrying about whether I would go to France or not was a good problem to have. There was so much in my life to be grateful for. I had a good life. I could feel it then sitting in the waiting room— my strong, healthy body, all the different species and genera of love radiating around my life, the pleasures of supermarkets and park benches and popcorn. And compared to this abundance, there was something petty about how much I resented the restrictions imposed on my passport. I was not an undocumented immigrant living in fear of police in the United States. I was not a Palestinian who had to subject herself to inspection in her own land. I was not an innocent man in Guantanamo.

My own taste of passport powerlessness was only a tiny glimpse of the enormously lopsided world that people with the wrong passports live in. An entire universe of people waiting for documents that may or may not come, now or never. Only now, after years of reading the history of passports and reading between the lines of this history, do I realize how directly connected these systems are.

After India secured its independence from the United Kingdom, for two decades, from 1947 to 1967, the newly independent Indian state would provide passports only to those citizens it deemed capable of representing India abroad. Naturally the passport system it put in place in order to ensure that only qualified Indians could travel abroad was based on the prevailing notions of caste and class. Kalathmika Natarajan, a historian of passports, writes of how the "international" became a space of anxiety where India's reputation had been besmirched by the shame of some of the earliest Indian migrants—indentured "coolies." The "coolie" had become a metaphor for an India that had been colonized and emasculated, and, newly independent and determined to erase this reputation, the country sought to prevent the travels of any Indian person who might embarrass it abroad. So, in addition to the hoops of educational qualifications and financial guarantees, bureaucrats were also encouraged to use the arbitrariness of their discretion to exclude anyone who had the potential to bring dishonor to the nation-state abroad. Natarajan notes the many euphemisms that Indian policy at the time used to avoid naming caste and class: *unskilled, undesirable, pedlar class*: words that were both laughably vague and subtextually precise.

•

Three days before our flight to France, as I was teaching an afternoon class, I got a mysterious text message from a strange number: "Your case status has been updated. Please check online." I forwarded the text to Rollo. His reply came back in seconds, in all caps: "APPROVED!"

The Advance Parole had been mailed out from a Missouri office. Would it reach us in time? It was Wednesday evening when we got the message, and the flight was on Saturday. The last possible day that I could get a French visa was Friday.

On Thursday morning, we called our local post office. "Sorry," they told us, "there is nothing from Missouri for that address."

I called the French consulate. "Madam, speak up please. No Advance Parole, no visa. No. No. No printouts from the website. I don't care if it has been approved. You cannot come late. We cannot wait for your mail, madam. What is that, madam? Speak up, please. You want to go to France, you must make Advance Parole."

Again, we called the post office. When we explained our situation, the post office manager, a woman who will get a rent-stabilized corner apartment in heaven when she dies, told us that we could come to the post office early in the morning on Friday so we could pick up our mail before our 10:00 a.m. interview at the French consulate.

The next morning, we arrived early at our post office. It hadn't opened yet. We paced outside in the chilly fall morning, holding hands. At 8:45 a.m. we walked up to the door and noticed a very tiny sign saying that the post office was closed for repairs. Parcels could be picked up from an address three doors down. We ran there. The mailman was sorting packages.

"This is only for parcels," he told us. "All first-class mail is at Kosciuszko Street."

Before he finished the sentence, we were in a cab, on our way to the real post office. "Can you wait for us outside? We will need to go to the French consulate right away," Rollo told the driver.

Inside the Kosciuszko Street post office, the kindhearted manager remembered us immediately. "So you are looking for mail from the Department of Homeland Security? Right, let me go get it."

Rollo put his arm around me and kissed my hair. A woman waiting in line smiled at us. I smiled back. Young lovers! Going to Paris tomorrow! The post office manager walked toward us with a long envelope.

She shook her head and said, "I am sorry." The envelope was not from the Department of Homeland Security.

Everyone was terribly sorry. "We regret that we cannot be of assistance to you in this regard," the ticketing agent from Air France told me after I canceled our expensive nonrefundable tickets later that day. My Advance Parole would arrive on Saturday, a day too late for my feeble Indian passport.

Rollo called from work a few hours later. "How are you doing?"

"Great! It's just money, you know," I said.

"Do you still want to go to Eid dinner?"

Of course I had forgotten all about the Eid dinner. Eid had fallen earlier that week, and we had made plans to attend Eid dinner at a community gathering in Times Square on Friday night. But after a sleepless night poring over my French visa application and a morning of running around, the thought of dressing up and talking to people seemed exhausting.

"We don't have to go," Rollo said. "The tickets were just twenty dollars each."

That was it. "We can't just keep buying tickets to things and not showing up," I snapped into the phone. "I'll see you at six."

And even though I had dragged us there because money didn't grow on trees, somehow Eid dinner managed to be fun. There was a *Jeopardy!* game based on the Qur'an. A kind older lady insisted on feeding me multiple helpings of baklava "for the baby." Most of all, how restorative to spend a few hours not thinking about not going to Paris.

As we were leaving the building, we heard music coming from the auditorium on the first floor. We peeked in, and then, somehow, we ended up sitting in the front row of a church open mic. The building the mosque was in housed various religious organizations, and a bunch of teenagers from the youth ministry of a local church were having a Friday-night social a few floors below the Eid dinner. And because we were not yet parents, because we had, for the last time in our life, nowhere to be, we joined the audience.

Someone had to support the amateur stand-up-comedian industrial complex.

"Our next musicians, I found them busking next to the carousel in Bryant Park and told them they should come to our open mic," the emcee said. "So here they are, Jean-François and Augustin, from Quebec."

Jean-François had a long mop of golden corkscrew curls and a colorful scarf knotted around his neck. Augustin was lanky and shy, his cap obscuring a birdlike head. The moment they started performing, it was clear that these two had outclassed everyone in the room. After a few tentative notes on Augustin's harmonica, they were off, Jean-François keeping time on accordion. Stories tumbled out through their instruments. Feet started tapping, bodies started swaying.

After a couple of songs, Jean-François pulled the mic toward him. "Er . . . zank you." His accent was so over-the-top that we all laughed. And he laughed with us. "If you want to take a piece of us home, we have CDs for sale. And if you really want to take us home, you can take us home because we need a place to stay tonight." Then it was time for a performance art piece about heartbreak involving a piano and a fork.

"Where would you have stayed last night?" I asked them the next day over breakfast.

"We go to café and stay awake the whole night and then in the morning, we sleep in the park."

Music students from Montreal, Jean-François and Augustin were taking time off from school to travel around the United States, playing songs and forming impromptu bands with other wandering musicians. They had gotten used to sleeping on park benches, in McDonald's, in the living rooms on couchsurfing.com. But New York had bewitched them, and they had decided to stay here for a couple of months.

"What will you be doing? Are you going to get jobs?" I asked.

"To make music is our job," Augustin replied.

"It is also our passion, so it does not feel like job." Jean-François flashed his killer smile. He picked up the Paris guidebook that was lying on the table. "You go to Paris soon?"

I summarized the Paris trip. Advance Parole. Visa appointment. Nonrefundable flight. Blah blah blah. Even as I told the story, I could hear how boring it was. *Is there a plot? Where is the drama? How anticlimactic.* It is impossible to tell a good story in which your primary antagonist is paperwork. That is the astuteness of using bureaucracy as a weapon of mass oppression. Our stories end up sounding like strings of bad luck rather than the result of a calculated move to stop peasants from coming to Paris.

Especially to two sweet white Canadians who were bouncing around the United States, making music, indifferent to borders and application forms. After they left to play music at the farmers market near our apartment, I thought of how the day before, as we were returning home with them, both of them declined when I offered them my MetroCard, instead swinging their legs and instruments over the turnstiles, gracefully evading the fare.

I was impressed. Every time someone evades a fare in the subway, my heart thrills with pride on their behalf. But somewhere within the admiration I save for this kind of recklessness, there is also a touch of resentment. What would it be like to commit a minor misdemeanor without worrying about how the color of my skin would be treated by the justice system? How would the world be different if smart, curious young people everywhere had the same opportunities to travel and take chances and sleep on park benches without being considered a public charge? Our young friends would have been horrified to hear about the *Komagata Maru*, yet the delicious freedoms they were enjoying and my own aborted travels were all historically connected.

This was when I began to consider renouncing my throne. After all, it's just a chair, really.

This is how one takes a defeat and begins to rationalize it into a kind of achievement. The Canadian writer David Rakoff wrote that the desire to become American comes over one suddenly, "not unlike that of the pencil-necked honors student suddenly overwhelmed with the inexplicable urge to make a daily gift of his lunch money to the schoolyard tough." It didn't come over me suddenly, it came over me gradually, but it too was a gift to a bully.

More accurately for me, it was a question of which bully to propitiate. Writing this in 2023, I am watching India turn into a fascist state where the repression of Muslims has become so casual and ordinary that a killing or two does not even make a news headline. Perhaps it's healthier to propitiate a bully whom you are not emotionally attached to. All I feel is the cold relief of someone who made a lucky bargain.

Besides, the question of what citizenship means goes to the heart of a question that is slowly brewing existential momentum: What is even a country? In a world where climate change is certain to wipe out low-lying island countries and create a whole new class of stateless people, a passport is increasingly a transactional commodity rather than a national identity. I do not see my story as a story of finding a new nation, about becoming American. I see myself as part of the transnational movement of people who acquire passports with a calculating eye on the benefits it can accrue. We are not motivated by nationalistic feelings or cultural affinity. Some of us are wealthy, like the billionaires who shop around for passports that will decrease their tax liabilities, and some of us are broke, like the Bidoon of the United Arab Emirates, a nomadic people for whom the government of Dubai bought Comoros passports, and some of us are in the middle, boringly middle-class with our aspirational fantasies of travel and civil liberties. In other words, I am not so different from the billionaires who shop for the most convenient citizenships, except, of course, for the billions.

A few hours later, Jean-François and Augustin knocked on our door, having lugged their accordion up four flights of stairs for the second time in twelve hours. This time, they were also loaded down with vegetables: broccoli, squash, potatoes, purple carrots, eggplants, brussels sprouts, beets. All the bounty of a farmers market in fall.

"We thought, since you cannot go to Paris, maybe we bring Paris to you. So we are going to cook you dinner and play music, and you can pretend you are in bistro in Paris," Jean-François says, eyes dancing.

"If you like," Augustin added prudently.

Jean-François held up two small yellow cylindrical objects. "Look, we got you candles. It will be very romantic, like Paris."

I knew these candles. They were beeswax candles from our favorite farm stand. They are not cheap.

"I hope you guys didn't spend all your money on this," I told Augustin.

"Pas problem. We made some money playing and we sold some CDs," he replied.

And so that night, when we should have been in Paris, we ate vegetables from upstate New York. Jean-François paced around our tiny kitchen smelling herbs and spices, pouring in way more olive oil than strictly necessary, flipping the pan and making the vegetables dance while Augustin cleaned up as they went. They served us on our own chipped and mismatched plates, inherited from generations of roommates. Fresh dandelion greens, caramelized peppers and zucchini and beans, dabs of goat cheese, and a cup of beet-red quinoa nestling in the middle. After we ate, Jean-François put a strawberry-rhubarb pie in the oven and took his accordion out. As the strawberry filling oozed out of the pie and filled the apartment with the smell of sun and butterflies and flowers, Jean-François and Augustin played French waltzes for us. And tango. And old jazz melodies.

And klezmer music. And then French waltzes again, because, after all, this was supposed to be a Parisian evening. We danced awkwardly, laughing at ourselves, our unborn child in between us. I looked at my husband—a man who has voluntarily performed onstage in an adult diaper—and I thought, *What fun it will be to raise a child with you, what a good life we have ahead of us.* And so we danced, hoping that the finicky neighbor downstairs wouldn't come pounding on our door because the music was too loud, too abundant. And my heart melted like a beeswax candle.

Chapter

THREE

MY FATHER HATES TRAVEL. HE ADMITS THIS FREELY, with no shame or guilt. When he hears about other people's road trips, he shakes his head sorrowfully, wishing they had more common sense. There's only one place in the world where he can get a good night of sleep and that is his own bed, which is a decades-old coir mattress that he has worn down to the appropriate firmness, like a Birkenstock sole. My father's greatest pleasure is to be at home reading news online and eating rice and coconut chammanthi every day. Ideally, the coconut should be from his village in Pathanamthitta District, southern Kerala, India.

Unfortunately, all his children live in other countries. One by one, we left behind our Kerala childhoods for school, for work, to join a spouse, to make a family. My sister and brother now live in the United Arab Emirates and I live in the United States, and thus our own family is no longer United in one place.

Every few months, my brother will send my parents a nonrefundable COK-DXB-COK ticket. My father's reluctance to travel will battle with his parsimony and my mother's determination to see her children. Eventually, he will board the flight, bundled up thoroughly against air-conditioning, which he hates almost as much as travel. Once he arrives at my brother's house in Dubai, he refuses to stir as much as possible. He knows what he likes: reading news. The Internet has brought him a bottomless newspaper to read every day. Someone has to read it all. Also, what could possibly be more interesting? When he does go out, it is usually for Friday prayers followed by lunch at one of the hundreds of Kerala restaurants in Dubai or Sharjah. In this way, he has managed to resist the terrible fate of doing something unfamiliar.

Outside these annual exiles, my father has made two international voyages. As soon as my parents could afford it, they went on the hajj pilgrimage to Makka, a journey mandated for every Muslim who has the health and means to do so. The other journey was a visit to New York to see his granddaughter.

When my daughter was a few months old, my father steeled himself for the ritual humiliation of the United States–visa interview, the eighteen-hour flight, and airplane coffee. They arrived on a fall evening in New York, on the same flight as Radiohead, which meant that my husband was busy staring open-mouthed at the band as they left the airport while his in-laws wandered around Arrivals, culture shock having been activated at the baggage carousel. (Five dollars for a luggage trolley? What kind of mafia runs this place? Etc.)

Somehow they made it to my living room with all eight pieces of luggage. My father immediately wanted to excavate his favorite coffee powder and drink a real cup of coffee. But before he could reach the suitcase, he was asleep on the couch. I couldn't help feeling slightly victorious. My parents had always been skeptical about the strange hours I kept in the first few days of coming home to them from New York. They would joke about the way I was up all night, raiding the fridge, and then falling asleep just as the household woke up. They were embarrassed when guests came to visit and were told at eleven in the morning that I was asleep. Jet lag seemed to them some kind of American double-talk, like invading a country for its oil and calling it democracy. But now here they were, fast asleep at three in the afternoon.

While my parents were in New York, I started freelancing for the United Nations as a writer of press releases. My job was to attend meetings of various General Assembly committees, listen to hundreds of delegates, and write coherent summaries that were circulated online. Governments read these summaries with a cold eye on how their positions were represented, counting the number of sentences given to their adversaries.

Every day the topics were different. I was working full-time after a long time and catching up on world news after months of relentlessly scouring parenting blogs. So I would wake up early in the morning to read up on the meeting topics of the day. My father, jet-lagged and out of sorts from sleeping on a soft bed, would be up already. He would make us coffee. While the rest of the household slept, I would pick his brain: "Tell me everything about the Western Sahara problem." Without batting an eye, he would give me the whole story, many decades' worth of reading international news, from both mainstream and alternative sources, condensed and articulated into his elegant and precise English. "What is happening in Gibraltar?" "Malvinas or Falkland Islands?" Every single time, he had nuanced answers. No offer of aid or proclamation of threat passed him by without a recounting of the submerged histories that had led to that point.

It was during those early morning conversations that I started realizing that there are many, many ways to travel. For years and years, my father had been traveling in exactly the way he wanted. He had been obsessively reading world news, scanning its politics and geography and the shifting landscape of squabbles, borders, allegiances. In this, he is very much a product of Kerala, a place where barbershops and bus stations ring out with intense conversations about international politics. But even among the argumentative Malayalis I grew up with, he stands out with his hunger for getting to the root of an issue, for reading multiple perspectives on the same debate, for forming informed opinions not for the sake of impressing friends and employers but for the sake of informed opinion.

The critic Benjamin Moser writes about the writer Machado de Assis, who lived a quiet and provincial life in nineteenth-century Brazil, "Machado is proof that cosmopolitanism comes from reading, not from travel: through books he knew the world." A certain kind of provincial can often be much more cosmopolitan than many world travelers. More often than not, this provincial is to be found in the Third World, where the hardship of getting visas and the financial inequalities between formerly colonial and colonized nations means that travel is out of reach, while reading is not. We often blithely say that reading is a passport to the world. For those whose passports carry the stigma of a Third World citizenship, reading is often the more accessible passport.

But reading is not simply a fat-free, gluten-free version of travel. Reading the world is, for the provincial, an act of self-preservation. People in Kochi and Rio cannot afford to believe in their exceptionalism. It would be pointless for them to pretend that they are isolated from the world or that they come first in the world. A butterfly wing flapping in Geneva or Rome or London or Washington, D.C., could well decide the fate of hurricane recovery on an island thousands of miles away. The current dominance of Western culture means that one does not have to travel to the West to find it, so non-Western cultures have learned to live alongside it, carefully assessing its predatory nature while attaining fluency in its tropes.

I have learned to respect this particular brand of worldliness that hinges on making sense of a precarious world, rather than enjoying the spoils of war. In his essay "Defining a New Cosmopolitanism: Towards a Dialogue of Asian Civilisations," the Indian critic Ashis Nandy writes: "It is possible to argue that Asia, Africa, and South America are the only cultural regions that are truly multicultural today. Because in these parts of the world, living simultaneously in two cultures—the modern Western and the vernacular—is no longer a matter of cognitive choice, but a matter of day-to-day survival . . ." Nandy points out that Western dominance has increasingly reduced the Western imperium to a provincial, monocultural existence. World domination comes at a price. This is the paradox by which European and North American cultures are increasingly losing their cosmopolitanism, because their definition of cosmopolitanism hinges on the universality of their own culture, from its version of coffee to its brand of human rights. On the other hand, the quiet, calculating cosmopolitanism of the non-Western provincial takes care to disguise itself as non-cosmopolitanism, to camouflage itself like an Amazonian butterfly. It takes on more layers of subversiveness the farther it moves away from the center.

Kerala is particularly fertile with this kind of camouflaged cosmopolitanism. In *The Adventures of Ibn Battuta*, a marvelous book that describes the world that Battuta traveled through in the fourteenth century, the historian Ross E. Dunn writes of the worldliness of Muslim minorities in the Indian Ocean world during the time that Battuta spent among them. "Simply to be a Muslim in East Africa, southern India or Malaysia in the fourteenth century was to have a cosmopolitan frame of mind," he writes, noting that being minorities, the Muslim communities in these regions felt deeply invested in preserving their links with the wider cultural world of Islam. Further, these communities were concentrated in coastal towns and dependent on maritime trade relationships. Often the inhabitants of these coasts responded more intensely to one another's political affairs than to what was happening in their own hinterlands.

Seven centuries later, this is still true of Kerala, where, according to cynical local wisdom, when the Arab Gulf countries catch a cold, Kerala sneezes. For me, as a child growing up in the 1990s in India, the Iraq-Kuwait war of 1991 was not a distant world event; it had ripple effects in my own neighborhood and school, when thousands of Malayali migrants suddenly had to flee Kuwait and their children turned up in the middle of the school year to join our classrooms. We grieved with the Palestinians as their lands were taken away and their protesters were shot at and their children shut away in military prisons for throwing stones. To be a minority is to constantly orient yourself against the world. Around the world, the people of small coastal Third World towns have a vested interest in the world. They are curious about how it works and does not work. It's a curiosity often missing in far-richer regions in the First World, whose inhabitants have the resources to travel but in ways that ensure that they can stay insulated from complicated historic, political, and economic sub-texts. We are led to believe that cosmopolitanism comes from tourism, from the ability to tick items off a bucket list or stick a colorful tack on a pushpin "conquest" map, but, in fact, migration and minorityhood is a more effective education in worldliness.

And so for my father, reading is not a substitute for travel. Reading is travel. Reading is how he understands the world. And there is nothing he likes reading as much as the international section of a newspaper. His mother loved newspapers. Even when his family fell on hard times, when crops dried up and fields had to be sold to pay her hospital bills, she would not give up her newspaper subscription. Every day she would quiz my father and his sister on the news stories of the day.

My father was born in a newly independent India. He came of age in the second half of the twentieth century. The Third World was shaking off colonial and feudal overlordship; the promises of democracy and freedom hung tantalizingly in the air right alongside the sulfur smell of bankrolled coup d'etats and instigated civil wars and partitions that redrew entire chunks of the map. Within many freshly minted nations, like India, communal and caste privilege reasserted itself, rising to occupy the seats freshly vacated by colonial rulers. The attention with which my father read the news—the first draft of history—is the watchfulness of someone who understands that knowledge is not power.

During those early morning conversations in New York, my father and I bonded deeply over chicory coffee and our shared disgust for the United Nations Security Council. In my growing-up years, we had fought so much, both of us argumentative and sarcastic. Now as we reflected on who gets to speak for nations and who doesn't, what gets left out of press releases, I appreciated his long memory, his epic view of world affairs.

But he refused to see any sights. Even New York City could not shake my father's desire to not see the world. He begged off the usual adventures to the Statue of Liberty, Times Square, Empire State Building. "It's not the Grand Canyon," he would say jokingly whenever I suggested sight-seeing. This was his "joke"—that there was only one thing he wanted to see in the United States: the Grand Canyon, which was conveniently far away.

While my parents acted as if they had flown eighteen hours around the globe to cook multicourse South Indian meals and sing lullabies, I wanted to show off the city on whose fortifications I had chiseled my little hollow. One day I surprised my parents with a helicopter tour over Manhattan. My mother got off the copter with windswept hair and shining eyes. "Just wonderful. What a way to see New York," she told me. My father shook his head and muttered, "Eminently avoidable."

But he loved grocery shopping in Brooklyn. Every day he would go to the Caribbean stores on Flatbush Avenue, near my home. My father didn't so much buy vegetables as investigate them. He was intrigued by the profusion of bananas, since these are not indigenous to the United States. He looked up Caribbean banana plantations and started reading about the history of the unequal trade between the United States and the region.

He also loved picking through my farm-share vegetables. It was fall, and week after week, our fruit share consisted of apples, a fruit that is rare and expensive in Kerala. Every Saturday, I sighed as we picked up yet another bushel of apples. I was tired of them but my father was not. He was mystified by this idea of getting bored. How can you be bored with good fruit? He ate all our apples and then started reading about different apple varieties.

It occurred to me then that my father has a wonderful sense of what the French call *terroir*. In Kerala, he is known to pick through several market stands to find the freshest kappa (cassava). He can spot a good bunch of kappa from a speeding car and will stop at roadside stands if the color and the shape catch his eye. He can tell by sight what kind of soil they were grown in.

Cassava is not native to Kerala. A product of the Columbian Exchange, it traveled to the west coast of India with Portuguese and Spanish colonizers, who encountered it first in Brazil. But today, soft and creamy boiled kappa is a beloved Malayali food. My father grew up surrounded by spindly kappa trees. When he finds good kappa, he will eat it for breakfast, lunch, and dinner till it is gone. The same with mangoes. When my mother's mango tree blooms in April, my father eats nothing but mangoes for dinner. "This is how I get my vitamin C," he tells us when we laugh at him.

In my family, we think of my father as someone with very limited tastes in food because he refuses to eat sliced bread, biscuits, candy, noodles, frozen packaged mishmash, anything out of a can. When I made my first cake out of a boxed mix, he took one bite and said guardedly, "It's very good. Please don't make it again." While we prided ourselves on being adventurous for trying out various processed crap, my father has always stuck to kappa and mangoes and coconut chammanthi. Watching him enjoy these apples, I realized that what he lacked was not curiosity; it was the ability to pretend to yourself that bad food tastes good.

So much of travel can be about pretending. I should know, because for years, I have been pretending to enjoy the monuments I visit in various places. I have spent perfectly sunny mornings in museums that I do not care for, and I have sat in cute trolley cars and I have thrown coins into wishing wells, all for the sake of ticking off an experience on a list. I have especially tried hard to enjoy walking tours. There are always good arguments for doing new things, and, having made them all to myself, I am now beginning to see the case for doing only the things you are genuinely curious about. As I grow older, I hope to become more like my father, who caused much amusement by declining a ride by the White House ("Why? What is there?") when we went to D.C. to visit my in-laws. When I told him my mother-in-law was offering to take him and my mother around D.C. on a guided tour of its monuments, he murmured sheepishly in my ear in Malayalam, "If the possibility of not going is not offensive, then that is the one that I would probably choose."

In the years since, I have been testing out my father's attitude to travel. When we arrive in a new place, I do my best to resist the iconic. For a people pleaser such as I am, this is difficult. Nevertheless, I try. When I hear of fun walking tours, I tell myself, *Eminently avoidable.* The truth, the frightening and liberating truth, is that nothing in the world is must-see or must-eat or must-do. It's all eminently avoidable, isn't it.

Instead, I shop for groceries and daydream in urban

parks, activities that I can enjoy without leaving Brooklyn, where I live. I skip the major monuments in favor of used bookstores and the small urban places of worship whose doors are usually propped open. But of course, this too is a fantasy—that by skipping the tourist trail, we can become travelers or even locals. It is only one slippery slope away from the iconic to the ironic.

My father's aversion to monuments is not a principled position against tourism. He is not trying to be a tourist, but he is also not trying to not be a tourist. Unlike Claude Lévi-Strauss, who famously begins his memoir, *Tristes Tropiques*, with "Travel and travelers are two things I loathe—and yet, here I am, all set to tell the story of my travel expeditions," my father does not dislike tourists. He does not notice them because travel as a form of self-improvement has not registered in his imagination. He loved what he loved—the halal street-food vendors, the Occupy Wall Street protests in Zuccotti Park—not because they were important but because they pierced through his indifference. In fact, he would be mystified to find himself in a book about travel. "Why?" he would probably ask. "What is there?"

I have tried hard to emulate this philosophical balancing act but with little success. Something has corrupted me too much. Over the years of saying no to things and refusing to try out other people's adventures, my father has managed to retain his triangularity in a world of round pegs with well-rounded to-do lists of travel experiences. Whereas I have said yes too many times.

I recognize myself in Dean MacCannell's 1976 classic *The Tourist: A New Theory of the Leisure Class*, in which he declares that the tourist is the key to understanding modern social structure. "Moderns somehow know what the important attractions are, even in remote places," MacCannell writes, calling tourism a "miracle of consensus" that works like a loop. While institutional mechanisms such as tourism agencies and travel guidebooks sacralize tourist sights, tourists respond by ritualizing the act of visiting these sights. He quotes the sociologist Erving Goffman, for whom "modern guided tours are extensive ceremonial agendas involving long strings of obligatory rites."

This religion of tourism, its holy books and its rituals, is deep within me even when I strike out on supposedly non-touristy paths. I am like the Jewish atheist in the famous joke who recoiled in horror after his son went to Catholic school and reported back about the Father, the Son, and the Holy Spirit: "Son," he responded, "there's only one God and He doesn't exist!" My aversion to tourism is a kind of faith in its power. *Nothing in the world is a must-see*, I told myself, while slowly roasting under the Roman sun in a two-hour line to step inside the Colosseum. *Nothing at all, except here I am.*

Why can't I simply shake off this faith in seeing places and things? As MacCannell writes, "the position of the person who stays at home in the modern world is morally inferior to that of a person who 'gets out' often." Traveling enables the modern to break the bonds of their everyday existence and begin to live. Perhaps you, too, have been told by some superior friend to "live a little" when you declined to go on a half-baked weekend trip. It is as if our everyday life is a pointless exercise and only when we travel do we reach our full potential. In fact, we are told, not only does travel make us better people; it makes the world a better place: a win-win. Travel has been sold to us as the ultimate horizon-expanding, mind-broadening, self-improvement experience.

In reality, of course, for many of us, travel has rarely been an uncomplicated pleasure. And as the climate emergency in which we are living moves toward its peak, it is getting harder to claim that travel is an uncomplicated good. Even the most hardened of us cannot ignore how travel is changing ecosystems, how travel has rendered so many places in the world into Disneyfied versions of themselves.

You know this already. I do too. Nevertheless, my inbox is full of cheap-fare alerts. Every day I am tempted by $300 New York City–Mallorca mistake fares. I will find ways to rationalize a stay in a luxury hotel that is slowly destroying the natural and cultural environment around it. Because of course I am not like other tourists. I deserve to travel because I am me, the right kind of traveler. Just as modern tourism is a parody of itself, anti-tourism too has become a parody of itself. And we can always convince ourselves that tourism is, for many Third World countries, the primary source of income. So many people count on our tourist dollars and dirhams and rupees.

Both these high moral grounds—tourism is terrible for the world, tourism is the best way to change the world—are

terribly hard on the knees and shins. Having lost my footing on both again and again, I am more interested now in
the low moral ground, which is located somewhere between
absolute apathy and an obsession with purity. It is the place
where one makes compromised choices and lives with some
regrets and celebrates small victories, while muttering to
oneself.

It's been years since that month my father spent in New
York City against his wishes. Every time I broach the topic
of another visit, he shudders. The flight is long, his patience
is short. But I want to take him apple-picking upstate. If he
comes again, we will definitely go to the Grand Canyon, I
assure him. "Even the Grand Canyon is not the Grand Canyon," he told me once, laughing heartily at his own joke.
While I waited for his laughter across the oceans to subside,
I remembered my favorite Cavafy poem, one that struck
terror into me when I was younger and dreaming about
other cities:

> You shall not find new places; other seas
> You shall not find. This place shall follow you.
> And you shall walk the same familiar streets,
> And you shall age in the same neighborhood,
> And whiten in these same houses.

The winter months are too cold; the summer months are
too hot; fall is when my parents go to Dubai. "Come to New
York in spring," I tell my father. "The weather is perfect,
with flowers everywhere." But April is when the mango tree

in my mother's garden blooms and sends ripe fruit pelting down on my parents' perennially bruised car. If he comes in April, how will my father stock up on vitamin C?

"No," he always responds. "You come here."

Chapter

FOUR

●→

AFTER MY PARENTS WENT BACK TO INDIA, AFTER MY husband's paternity leave dried up, there came the terrifying moment when it was just the baby and me. A normal day in modern motherhood; an awful aberration in the history of child-raising.

So much of a new parent's life is spent latching buckles. Where there used to be multiple hands, we now have belts and gates and harnesses. But someone still has to clamp them in place. Just like that, I had been evicted from my own life and placed on a strange new planet that was administered by the bureaucracy of motherhood. Time itself changed. A day became something to trudge through. The tight, tired feeling in my lower back became a permanent fixture. I tried yoga. I tried therapy. I tried the Baby Clay class. I tried more coffee. I had many sweet moments with my baby, but nothing was as sweet as the relief I felt when my husband returned from work and took the baby over.

Finally, one bleak winter morning, some elemental instinct made me get out of the apartment with the baby in a sling and walk to the nearest corner and get on a city bus. It was going toward the riverfront in Brooklyn. That sounded like a fine place to be. When we got there, though, I realized I didn't particularly want to be there. Where I wanted to be was on the bus, watching the world go by.

Thus, I discovered, the wheels of the bus go round and round, round and round, round and round, all over town. Soon this became a habit. It didn't matter what bus or where it was going. Dazed from lack of sleep, I would walk out of my apartment building with the baby snug against me and make for the bus stop. If there was a bus at the corner, I would get into it. If not, I would walk to the next corner and catch whatever bus happened to stop there. It was like climbing onto a carousel. The bus itself was my destination as long as it was empty enough that I could score a window seat. For a couple of dollars and change, my baby and I had a warm hour or two and a ladleful of Brooklyn Stew. The bus was a moving theater. But a very low-stakes theater, one in which you could watch the play, slip into your thoughts, lose the plot thread, and then return to the play and still somehow make sense of it. A woman walks into a shoe shop. An old lady pushes a cart into a supermarket with discounts plastered all over the windows. A security guard outside a dollar store is laughing on his phone but changes his expression briefly to look sternly at a man walking out. Suddenly there was so much to see.

At first I was just grateful to not be in Baby Clay class. Any of the many hours that I spent bus-hopping was livelier than the forty-three excruciating minutes I once spent watching three infants (including mine) drool into Play-Doh while the adults made awkward conversation about moving or not moving to the right school districts. I did feel a bit guilty climbing into the bus. Back in the apartment, there were always dirty dishes. But it was not just the undone chores. A modern baby's life is as culturally demanding as a Jane Austen heroine's. She needs to draw, paint, and play the piano. Instead here was my baby staring out through a foggy bus window and then drooping off to sleep, lulled by the hum of an internal combustion engine. I consoled myself by imagining how a big toy manufacturer would have marketed this ride: "Engage your baby's cognitive and social skills with a bus ride today! The window will provide her a constant diorama of scenes that will activate her reasoning, memory, and problem-solving. The occasional glimpses of her own reflection will trigger self-awareness. And when she is ready to sleep, the gentle rocking motion will remind your baby of the safest place on earth, your womb!"

•

Buses were useless to me until then. I had gone years without getting on a bus. If I was not taking the subway or biking, I walked. I don't know if this should be considered a hobby or a disorder, but going for a walk is my idea of a marvelous time. I love hiking, I love walking in the park, and I love street strolling. Of course, when I came upon the term *flaneur*, I fell upon it greedily—*What? There's a word for the kind of aimless wandering I love so much?*

Brooklyn, where I live, is a flaneur's paradise with its broad sidewalks. When I visit my parents in India, I frequently walk on the railway platform near their house, which feels akin to the promenades in many European cities. Few neighborhoods in Ernakulam have footpaths, but this does not mean that vehicles have the right-of-way. Instead, vehicles and pedestrians have joint custody of the road, and most of the time this custody is amicable. Still, the luxury of a broad sidewalk on which I can walk absent-mindedly is something I savor whenever I return to Brooklyn, with its tree-lined, dog-shit-strewn sidewalks.

Walking the city is a kind of reading. If the city is the text, the sidewalk/footpath/pavement is where we write our notes. Like many writers, I walked aimlessly and narcotically. In the middle of the day and late in the night. In the hell heat of Brooklyn summer and during its wicked winter. I have walked alone, crossing streets for no better reason than an amenable green light, climbing over abandoned riverside warehouses that would eventually be turned into glossy glass towers, pausing to ask directions because I was mesmerized by a face. I have walked with friends and lovers, drifting in and out of conversations and parks, bridging rivers of talk, back and forth.

On the other hand, if I actually needed to get anywhere, I took the subway. Like most New Yorkers, I had figured out exactly where to wait on the subway platform so that I could exit efficiently when going to work or coming home. There was nothing efficient about the bus. Once while walking down Broadway in Manhattan, I walked fifty-six blocks, outpacing the Broadway bus on each block as it paused in traffic or waited at traffic lights. Its slow, plodding ways were no use to me. But now, with a baby bundled against me, I was slow and plodding too. The bus and I were perfect for each other.

Often I watched and marveled at how unflappable the bus drivers were. On every block, the bus would stop two or three times—there's the scheduled stop, the inevitable red light, traffic backup, and, just when the road seems clear, someone will cross in the middle of the block. Like a monk watching a mandala being destroyed, the bus driver would brake again and again, face stoic. It was as if each interruption was expected. Or rather, the interruptions were also part of the journey.

•

Of course, the flaneur as imagined by Charles Baudelaire and Walter Benjamin and other great writer-flaneurs was male. In *Flâneuse: Women Walk the City in Paris, New York, Tokyo, Venice, and London*, Lauren Elkin writes about how women have been excluded from the history of walking our cities, how scholars have dismissed the idea of a female flaneur again and again. But the presence of the flaneur does not preclude the presence of flaneuses. Lynda Nead, in *Victorian Babylon: People, Streets and Images in Nineteenth-Century London*, shows that women were flaneusing in the streets of London as flaneuring came into existence as a modern activity. Baudelaire himself writes about the women he sees on the streets, from which we can assume that women were not only seen but also seeing. Elkin and

Nead argue that flaneuses have always existed; they were just made invisible by male readings of flaneury.

To that, I add this question: Is walking the only way to flaneur? If casual wandering and a love for the "infraordinary" are the hallmarks of the flaneuse, if it is an attitude to urban life above all, then perhaps a bus slowly slithering through the streets of Brooklyn can be a catalyst of flaneury, just as much as a café on a well-positioned corner. After all, what could be more infraordinary than the city bus? And who is more anonymous than a mother with a child? The presence of a child is like an invisibility cloak. Nothing to see here, just a mother and a child. The usual stuff. Humdrum. Men whose eyes would have lingered on us before look through us now. It is as if the borders of our selfhood are bleeding into the environment, turning us into background scenery. If we are out and about instead of at home, it must be for some boringly respectable errand like buying spinach or seeing a doctor.

In those limbo days of early motherhood, I pulled this invisibility cloak around me like a safety blanket. It was only after I became invisible that I fully realized the weight I had been carrying around as an object. The burden of looking busy and indifferent, fending off protection or attention. The weight of being constantly looked at. How freeing to no longer be an object. So this is what those male flaneurs were experiencing.

But, over the course of a century, something else has come to rest on *flaneuring/flaneusing*. The word has become loaded with a kind of sophistication I do not have.

It immediately brings to mind a Western über-metropole composed of the best bits of Paris, London, and New York. As if these cities have not been unsafe for the people on their margins. Maybe it is also because so much has been said about flaneury that I no longer feel comfortable claiming to be a flaneuse without reading twenty books and parsing definitions propagated by academics in at least six disciplines. This seems to miss the point of flaneuring, which was premised on an intimacy with streets and not JSTOR. Or maybe it is simply because I have never quite learned how to twist my tongue around the curves of the word *flaneur*.

•

There's a word in Malayalam for the kind of aimlessness I was indulging in: *vaynokkal*. Literally, it means "looking in the mouth"—I guess because what could be more pointless than staring into a mouth? *Vaynokkal* has many shades of meaning. Vaynokkal can be dreamy, a way to pin your gaze on something concrete while evacuating into your thoughts. Vaynokkal can also be alert, a thorough if pointless study of your surroundings. And sometimes vaynokkal can also be flirty, an opportunity to look and be looked at. The point is always the pointlessness. It is not self-improving in any way. It is a waste of time.

On the streets of my hometown, there were always clusters of vaynokkis, always men. Depending on the time of the day, they might be unemployed or underemployed, students or working men after their workday. They were also the men for whom the street was the workplace: food vendors, the auto-rickshaw and taxi drivers, the umbrella- and shoe-repair men who could be found under a shady tree near a bus stop. And there were those for whom the street itself was home: the urban poor who live on the margins of the margins. In an essay in the *Oxford Anthology of the Modern Indian City*, Arjun Appadurai, writing of the "organized idleness" of Indian streets, points out that hanging around is a highly cultivated aspect of Indian street culture. The streets may be filled with purposeful walkers and traffic patterns, but "there is always a steady audience of those who are in no hurry to go anywhere; they are just there to watch, perhaps to talk, perhaps to sell, but mainly just to pass the time."

Rarely are any of the organized idlers on small-town Indian streets women. A woman who pauses to simply pass the time would invite curiosity, much of it threatening. And while different cities have different degrees of curiosity about women on the streets, it is safe to say that every Indian woman learns early to put on a stone face while walking through crowded streetscapes. As a teenager running errands for my parents or waiting to catch the school bus, I learned to put on a good-girl mask of studied indifference while remaining alert to movements in my vicinity.

It was not just unsavory male attention that I knew I had to ward off; it was also the eagle-eyed family friend and the neighborhood aunties and uncles. In *Why Loiter?: Women and Risk on Mumbai Streets*, Shilpa Phadke, Sameera Khan, and Shilpa Ranade write about how a woman's right to loiter is a crucial building block for an equitable city. Another useful word—*loitering*. So close to littering and its suggestion of something that shouldn't be there. *Loitering* also brings to mind the lottery and the gamble of waiting for something to happen. The authors describe loitering as an act of pleasure-seeking that holds multiple delicious possibilities: expanding women's access to public space; transforming women's relationship with the city; reenvisioning citizenship in more inclusive terms. Their analysis is especially incisive in considering the ways in which restrictions on women's mobility are rationalized in relation to the presence of the "dangerous other": lower-class men and Muslim men. In fact, Phadke, Khan, and Ranade argue, such men are themselves the objects of surveillance. We need to rehabilitate this act of hanging out without purpose—not just for women, but for all marginal groups, they write, making a case for the right to "loiter without being asked what time of the day it was, why we were there, what we were wearing and whom we were with."

I love this idea of loitering as an embodied act of taking space *and* giving space, as opposed to the individualism inherent to flaneuring. The loiterer is aware of others on the margins of the streetscape and willing to share this space, making it a collective public good, as opposed to a vantage point from which to objectify the other. This spoke to me, especially within the peculiarly American loneliness of nuclear-family child-raising, trapped within the bureaucracy of regular naptimes and cribs and Baby Clay and family restaurants.

It certainly helped that Brooklyn's buses are full of immigrants from other countries whose attitude to babies in public places is one of hospitality. Fellow passengers made duck and cat noises, played peekaboo behind bulging shopping bags, and let little exploring hands touch their umbrellas and bags. And in turn, it didn't bother me at all when different passengers told me the baby must be cold, the baby must be overheating, the baby must be overdressed, the baby must be hungry, the baby must be tired. I understood it to be phatic: a stranger's way of saying, *I am a fellow human looking out for the youngest member of our tribe.* It takes a city to raise a child.

Especially during holiday season, the parenting sections of newspapers and magazines are full of articles about how to travel with children. How to entertain them on road trips and flights. What to pack. Which toys are the best for travel, with affiliate links embedded for your convenience. Some of this guidance is useful, and like those nineteenth-century travelers who turned to guidebooks because they did not have tutors, so many of us, raising children far away from our families, need this parenting wisdom. But after a certain point, the overflow of advice becomes the very thing that convinces us that a child cannot be deciphered or managed without this information. We start internalizing that the world outside is so dangerous and our children so willful that the encounter between the two must be controlled through entertainment and consumption.

Loitering in buses taught me that fellow travelers can always be trusted to offer you kindness and understanding. In the years that followed, rarely did I feel anxious about traveling anywhere in the world with a small child. A child unravels the self-centered individualism that modern travel encourages. The lovely strangers on the Brooklyn buses trained me to think of the world as a slow, gentle bus that we are all on.

I often thought of the travel writer Dervla Murphy, who has biked from Ireland to Delhi, fended off wolves in Yugoslavian forests, ridden a donkey through Ethiopia, and walked a mule through the Andes. She made some of these journeys with her child. Murphy was often questioned about the dangers of traveling with a child, but her response was that a child's presence makes travel easier. It emphasizes your trust in the community's goodwill. A child signals that you come in peace because a traveler with a child is vulnerable in ways that invite strangers to open toward them.

This is both true and false. We only have to think of the refugee families whose photos we have all become familiar with and all the others who did not make it to photos such as those. Middle and upper classes everywhere in the world have perfected the art of not seeing the refugee children, the homeless children, the children who live on the streets, the children who ask for more than we want to give. But when we turn away from a child who needs our help, we know we are turning away from our better selves. Children, for the most part, disarm the strangers within us.

I was, of course, neither appealing for asylum nor riding a horse across a snowcapped Andean mountain. There was no evidence for travel in my round-trip bus journeys. But I realize now that though I was sitting still in a bus in Brooklyn, I was journeying into a foreign land called motherhood. It's such a strange experience to be out in public with your child in the early days of parenting. For the world, you are another mother with her child. For you, the world is a new place, charged by the electricity of what has happened to you.

Around then, a mythology of Brooklyn was coming into shape. A friend in São Paulo, Brazil, was looking to move apartments. She told me that one of the apartment buildings she went to see was called "Brooklyn." A few months after I wrapped up my unpaid bus-hopping maternity leave, *The New York Times* reported that "among young Parisians, there is currently no greater praise for cuisine than 'très Brooklyn,' a term that signifies a particularly cool combination of informality, creativity and quality." Speeding through an Indian highway that summer when I visited family, I caught sight of a billboard for Brooklyn in Bangalore. Brooklyn had become a brand, a simulation, a mythology.

But the Brooklyn I saw from the window of the bus was anything but très Brooklyn. This Brooklyn was not on the gourmet-coffee map of Brooklyn that I spied one day in a coffee shop. At least not yet. Here in this other Brooklyn, where there were not yet any luxury apartment buildings or farm-to-table restaurants or vintage boutiques, the bus was king and queen. It went where the trains did not. It plodded down streets full of bungalows with peeling paint, avenues that were lined with Chinese restaurants and shops that sold all kinds of random things that had fallen off the backs of trucks, and church-basement soup kitchens. Many of the neighborhoods the bus passed through bore the names of old Dutch and British slave-owning settler families, but the fruit-and-vegetable stores, filled with callaloo and star fruit and pide bread, told another story.

Sometimes I stayed on the bus all the way to the end of the route and rode the return bus home. Sometimes I made up errands—return a book in another neighborhood branch of the Brooklyn Public Library, find a newspaper in a language I don't speak, buy a fruit that I have never seen before. From the leafy lulls around Prospect Park, the B16 took me to the hustle and bustle of commercial streets in Borough Park. The B35 skirted the borough like the sweep of the sun above, from Remsen Village in the east to the East River in the west, the pastoral names ironic against the gritty concretescape the bus traverses. The B41 picked up shoppers and schoolkids on the commercial stretch of Flatbush Avenue, then visitors to the park, the Botanic Garden, and the museum, before it crawled on Seventh Avenue toward artisan ramen.

One day, a woman got on a crowded bus. A big, older woman in a ragged jacket. She looked through her wallet and brought out one MetroCard after another. None of them worked. The driver curled his mouth and said, "The bus is not leaving till you pay the fare." In all my days of bus-hopping, this was the only time I saw a bus driver be cruel. Silently, the woman went through all her useless Metro-Cards again. "You need to get off the bus right now," the driver yelled, gratuitously since the bus was pin-drop silent by now. He switched off the engine and crossed his arms. Passengers sighed. The woman shuffled and pretended to search in the pockets of her threadbare jacket.

And then, the man sitting in the handicapped seat leaned

on his stick and arched forward and handed his MetroCard to the woman. She swiped it, the bus driver switched on the engine, and we were hurtling past the trees of Green-Wood Cemetery as they slowly broke green. Winter had lost the battle and spring was pushing its way through.

And if there is something to match the generosity of its people, it is the exquisite beauty of Brooklyn. My favorite time to be in a bus was the soft-spoken hour before the sun set. Gas stations and silent leafless trees and graffiti on the side of an ancient building and playgrounds with someone's water bottle left on a bench. On a block of creamy Victorian mansions, suddenly a bold red door. The parabolic curve of the bus as it rounded the corner on Avenue X. Nestling against a smooth bus seat, my beautiful little burden breathing on me, I felt transported, again and again and again.

Sitting on the bus going nowhere also brought back muscle memories of sitting in other buses in other places. The overnight buses of Turkey, where the conductor brings you instant coffee. The ring-road buses of Delhi that circle the city in a dusty loop, punctuated by gorgeous monuments. The bus ride in Uruguay along the coastal highway during which a vegan young woman cried on my shoulder telling me how European meat factories buy cows in Uruguay in order to circumvent EU animal-farming regulations. The bus from Phnom Penh to Siem Reap that unfortunately broke down along the way, fortunately at the most scenic spot possible. The bus from London to Oxford, from whose window I saw for the first time a Western suburb and felt the cold hand of anxiety that this is considered a decent way to live. All these memories intermingled with the clink of coins and MetroCard swipes and next-stop announcements.

•

Conversely, sitting in a city bus surrounded by the bustle of city life also reminded me how much I hated taking buses on U.S. highways. My husband and I would often take the bus to Washington, D.C., to visit his family. As soon as we found ourselves on the expressway, my mind would turn into rubber. I felt every minute of the four-to-five-hour journey. The minutes did not pass so much as drag themselves over the asphalt and air freshener and the bass of traffic.

I was surprised because I had believed what the books told me about the romance of the American highway. From the open road that called to Walt Whitman to the migrant workers on the mother road to California in John Steinbeck's Depression epic to the freewheeling escape from adulthood in Jack Kerouac's counterculture narrative, the shape and size of this fat country, sprawled from coast to coast, mountain to desert, lends itself to long, winding roads of self-discovery. But what I didn't realize until I got here and took my first bus ride is that those wide-open highways had given way to high-speed multilane expressways. About a decade after the publication of *On the Road*, Jack Kerouac tried to replicate the book's wild 1940s zigzag from New York City to San Francisco. He had to give up.

On the Road was published in 1957, six years after Kerouac wrote his first draft on a long scroll, a highway in

form, during three weeks in 1951. In 1956, President Dwight
Eisenhower approved the Federal-Aid Highway Act, which
authorized the building of forty thousand miles of interstate
expressways. The roads that Kerouac had improvised his
road trip on were rapidly replaced by the "broad ribbons"
that Eisenhower wanted to ensure that the military could
move quickly in case of the atomic attack that never came.
By the time *On the Road* was published, the death knell had
already been rung for the highways that Kerouac journeyed
on. There were also 30 million more cars on the roads.

Two decades after Kerouac's failed attempt to retrace his
travels, William Least Heat-Moon would go to great lengths
to avoid Eisenhower's broad ribbons as he road-tripped
around the country, avoiding expressways and taking back
roads whenever he could. So many of the incoherent resent-
ments I felt toward interstates became more intelligible to
me when I read his *Blue Highways*, the book that resulted
from this three-month odyssey. Having grown up a child of
the 1950s, Heat-Moon was there to witness the ways in which
the country changed as it switched from highways to expressways. "We believed the national defense argument until it became apparent the four lanes were there to move not
rifles but radios, not bombs but baubles; they were there to
sell autos, tires and gasoline; they were there to push public
transportation toward private transport, to give semi-trailer
trucks a publicly-paid-for right of way," he wrote elsewhere.

One of the casualties of the rapid expansion of expressways was Main Street, the arterial road of the American
small town. Main Street was where the town came to shop,

to get haircuts, to watch movies, to exchange library books, to stand at street corners and gossip. But as interstates bypassed towns, they sucked the mercantile life out of Main Streets and into their exit points, like "vacuums from hell," as Heat-Moon puts it. Another casualty was regional food: as speed limits increased, independent restaurants vanished, and with them went "hundreds of Mizzus Somebody's own blue-ribbon-at-the-county-fair recipe for corncob soup or nut pie à la Bama," "the scent of a farmer's loam after rain, the smell of a Gulf shrimp boat." With the onset of expressways, these were replaced by what Heat-Moon describes as "low-margin high-turnover polystyrene food"—a description that I can never unthink now.

It pops into my head and makes me shudder with gratitude every time I stop for meals or snacks during road trips in India. There is so much delicious food to be found along the highways of India, from the fish and toddy shops lined temptingly along national Highway 66, which runs along the west coast, to the dhabas that pockmark the shoulders of the Grand Trunk Road, food destinations in themselves. In more recent years, American-style rest stops with fast-food-franchise restaurants have been creeping up along these highways. Whether by invasion or imitation, American versions of infrastructure get exported throughout the world. This means that the kind of monoculturization that American interstates disseminate does not simply stay at home. It becomes the face of travel around the world. More and more people will travel in the future, for work and for play. As countries around the world invest in infrastructure to meet this demand, we need to learn from the exorbitant environmental, social, and cultural price that the United States has paid for privileging automobile culture over public transportation.

The beginning of the interstate era coincided with the decline of investment in public transportation, just when the civil rights movement had managed to achieve desegregation in buses and trains, Mia Bay writes, in *Traveling Black: A Story of Race and Resistance*. From the beginning, racism was baked into the asphalt of the expressway in multiple ways. The expressways helped fuel white flight into the suburbs even while redlining kept communities of color in the city. Blacks, Hispanics, and other people of color were carefully excluded from the suburban autopias that the interstates led to. This was not an accidental oversight. The Federal Housing Administration (FHA) routinely refused mortgages to Black people who attempted to buy suburban homes and maintained that neighborhoods occupied by "incompatible racial or social groups" were risky to invest in. The underwriting manual of the FHA recommended interstates as a good way to separate African American neighborhoods from white neighborhoods.

As my bus passed under the steady drone of the Brooklyn-Queens Expressway, I could see the way it had blighted that corner of Brooklyn, separating a primarily immigrant working-class community from a white neighborhood built around a neighborhood school and a sprawling park and a playground filled with white children. Policymakers such as Robert Moses often used interstates to break up and scatter neighborhoods they considered undesirable. Thus, the social and environmental cost of building an interstate was often borne by low-income neighborhoods populated by people of color, while the benefits—spacious houses, access to nature and outdoors, high-functioning schools, all the invisible tail-winds of living in a "good neighborhood"—accrued to white suburban neighborhoods. The interstate police patrols were also the first to operationalize racial profiling, a policy that began with the "war on drugs" and continued with the "war on terror." What is an experience of freedom and safety for white road-trippers was and continues to be a fraught encounter for Black people and people of color.

The most dangerous moment in all my travels anywhere in the world was in a rural suburb in upstate New York where I had gone to attend an extremely white wedding. I was walking down a country road early one morning when suddenly four huge dogs flew toward me, enormous white teeth flashing like in a movie close-up of wild animals. Just before they got to me, a white woman on a porch up the road called them off. I had wandered into her property, she shouted, from behind the barrel of a gun. Did I not see the sign saying PRIVATE PROPERTY, TRESPASSERS WILL BE SHOT?

As my bus moved through the bustling streets of Brooklyn, it moved through public property. Streets full of the vibrancy of human encounter. Street corners full of vaynokkis. The mingling of sound and smell to create new semantics. What I was looking at was Main Street, except spread out across the borough. Unlike expressways, many of which are increasingly built with enormous sound barriers that wall them off to contain noise pollution, the city bus moves through living communities. The world it moves through has not been standardized and franchised; it has room for the unexpected.

•

One day, we were on the second or third bus of the day when we caught the end of the school day. Like fish swimming downstream, they poured in, laughing, gossipy high school students, all bones and elbows and backpacks, their racial makeup spanning the breadth of the world. While one or two sat quietly doing their homework or pretending to, others made jokes, yelled and cursed, and played games. A girl in hijab psychoanalyzed a teacher. A group of boys burst into laughter and high fives every thirty seconds. And in one corner, a girl and boy held hands and talked to each other softly, though no one could have heard them anyway. I sat amid them, mammal among birds, and wondered which one of these my sleeping baby would be in ten, twelve, fourteen years.

The bus sped down the avenue, and I noticed something strange. The subway tracks above the ground in the distance, that ancient bakery at the corner—surely I had been here before. As far as I could tell, this was my first time on this bus route. But déjà vu gnawed at me. Where were we? The vagueness of the memory itched. Then I finally remembered. Years ago, I had walked down this very avenue to get my fingerprints scanned as part of my application for my green card. In the basement of a discount shopping mall, I had pressed my fingers onto a glass plate and recorded them for the Department of Homeland Security.

It had taken me several hours that day to get to this part of Brooklyn and I had wondered then, *Why is the application support center here?* I was annoyed by the long, fumbling ride, changing train after train, asking directions to people who misled me. Most of all, I was annoyed by myself. I had turned into an immigrant. I had proved him right, that video documentary guy who had announced, "People from the Third World do not travel. They immigrate." For so long, I had taken comfort in being an outsider in the United States. But there I was, marrying a U.S. citizen, auditioning to belong, begging to be included. And after all that, there was the anticlimax of the Application Support Center, which looked like a place where you go to get an illegal abortion. *What is it doing in this random, nondescript corner of Brooklyn?* I had grumbled to myself then. The bus now stopped around the corner from there.

The couple who were holding hands untwined and he got off. He stood on the corner, a skinny Hispanic boy, waving furiously at her, the Asian girl with braces. As the bus started moving off, he held his right hand close to his heart and then signed *I love you* with his fingers. And she smiled that adolescent metallic smile from the bus and signed back: *I love you.*

There are no random, nondescript corners in Brooklyn. Earth and air, glass and skin and bus—our fingerprints are everywhere.

Chapter

FIVE

✈

I FIRST HEARD ABOUT BILQIS, THE QUEEN OF SHEBA, IN A madrassa in Kerala. I was nine or ten years old, and we were reading the Qisas-el-Anbiya. The ustad was reading aloud the Malayalam translation of this medieval collection of stories from the lives of various prophets of Islam, of whom Suleyman was one. I was deeply struck by the wonderful brazenness of the women in the Qisas. Zulaykha trying to seduce Yusuf, Musa's mother secretly keeping him alive though the Pharaoh has commanded that all infants be killed, and now Bilqis, the queen of Sheba, setting off to see Suleyman for herself.

My favorite teacher—Ra'uf ustad—loved telling stories. Unlike the other ustads, he cracked jokes and laughed easily and did not spend most of the time telling the girls in the class we were fitnas. Ra'uf ustad told us that when she arrived in Jerusalem in Suleyman's court, the queen of Sheba was impressed by the pristine glass pavilion on which his throne was placed. Mistaking it for water, she lifted the hem of her skirts lest they get wet. In fact, Suleyman had the glass pavilion constructed to trick the queen into showing her legs. He had been told by djinns that she was a cloven-footed devil, and before he welcomed her into his court, he wanted to see for himself.

Years later, while traveling in Ethiopia, I came across a coda to this encounter between the queen of Sheba and Solomon. According to the Ethiopian epic Kebra Nagast, Sheba was a territory in what is now Ethiopia, and its Queen Makeda visited Solomon after hearing about his greatness. She won over his heart with her beauty and wisdom, and he tricked her into sharing his bed. They conceived a child, who went on to found the old Ethiopian empire of Aksum. Historians believe that the queen of Sheba could have belonged to what is now Ethiopia or one of its neighbors, Eritrea or Yemen. After all, one of the presents that the queen brought Solomon was frankincense, which grows only in this region.

But sitting in the madrassa all those years ago, when I heard of the queen of Sheba mistaking the glass pavilion for water, I was reminded of another story, another king. Dushasana, from the Hindu epic Mahabharata, visiting his cousins, the Pandava brothers, in their fancy new capital of Indraprastha. Dushasana too is tricked by a glass floor so pristine that he thinks it must be water and steps gingerly, causing another queen—Draupadi—to erupt into the laughter that will launch a long, bloody battle. Growing up, I was surrounded by the swirl of these ancient stories, and my head was the first melting pot I knew. At school, I learned the names of the great explorers of history—Magellan, Vasco da Gama, Columbus—and the dates on which they arrived in the lands they set out in search of. But in my head, the stories of prophets evicted from their cities and desert mothers in search of water and princes exiled from their kingdoms and monkeys leaping across oceans were also stories of travel and adventure.

It seems to me remarkable that we have, if only via myth, the story of a woman traveler from Africa before the beginning of the Common Era. She was a queen, a woman of great power and agency, which she used judiciously. Her confidence and curiosity are writ large all over the various versions of the story. According to the Hebrew Bible, she came to test Solomon with hard questions, and according to the Kebra Nagast, when Solomon, hatching a convoluted plot to trick her into sleeping with him, makes her promise not to steal anything from him, she informs him crisply that she is wealthy and has as much money as he does. None of these versions detail much about her journey to Jerusalem, which must have been arduous and uncertain. In fact, in one version of the story, it was djinns who transported the queen instantaneously to Jerusalem.

Can religious and mythological tales be considered travel records? Aren't they just stories? In his introduction to *Other Routes: 1500 Years of African and Asian Travel Writing*, Tabish Khair makes a strong case for considering epic poetry and religious texts as a form of travel writing. Travel, Khair points out, seems to mark the beginning of all major religions, from the exile of Ram in the Ramayana to the Buddha's wanderings after leaving behind the palace to the wayfarers of Daoism to Moses's return from Mount Sinai to Muhammad's journey before the revelation. The mixture of fact and fiction in such stories offers an early prototype of travel and travel writing, he writes, because through these narratives, the storytellers are discursively mapping their own selves against the other, home against the foreign.

Indeed, in the way the queen of Sheba observes Solomon and as the Old Testament describes it, "the house that he had built, the food on his table, the seating of his servants, the service of his waiters and their apparel, his cupbearers, and his entryway by which he went up to the house of the Lord," we see this discursive mapping of the self and the other. Herself a wealthy monarch, the queen of Sheba is taking stock of the difference between her and Solomon, and she is willing to give Solomon his due while taking her own.

Perhaps what delights me more than anything else is that the queen of Sheba's journey is a counterpoint to the monomyth that Joseph Campbell wrote about in his book *The Hero with a Thousand Faces*, in which every myth follows the template of a hero's journey that involves a man who journeys away from home, encounters monsters and temptations, and returns home with a prize. The queen of Sheba has all the prizes she wants at home—she is wealthy, she rules over her own kingdom, she has the love and loyalty of her people. What she is motivated by is curiosity.

As a child, I thrilled to imagine the queen of Sheba's travels because she was a woman. But over the years, I have come to think that what's truly subversive about her journey is her curiosity. Her desire to know, to understand, to see for herself is entirely different from the desire to capture, to defeat, to bring back a trophy.

Travel history insists that most ancient travel took place for war and trade, for securing prizes in one form or another. The first travel writing in recorded history is a story of military exploits. Herodotus, a Greek man, born in what is now Turkey, traveled all over the eastern Mediterranean and well beyond, documenting the rise and fall of the Persian Empire in the fifth century BCE. Right at the beginning, he informs the reader that he is writing a record of events so that the Greeks and the "barbarians" may receive their due. He called his account *historia*—little did he know that he was inventing a field of study (history) and a genre of storytelling (travel writing). Even today, both the field and the genre bear this Herodotean legacy of pitting one's imagined community against the "barbarian" other.

•

Here's another traveler: a man from Syria on his way to Europe, where he hopes to tell his story and win over the authorities there. He has fled Damascus and has been wandering since then from place to place talking to whoever will listen. Many have helped, but there has also been great hostility toward people like him. He has been beaten and arrested and evicted. Can you blame him for setting his sights across the seas? The men in the capitals of empires have so much power over people like him. So even though he knows all too well the prejudices against his faith, he hopes that maybe he will get a fair hearing, in another land. Or maybe he is thinking of future generations and what he owes to them as he sets out on this long and perilous journey. The ship he sails on makes a dangerous crossing of the Mediterranean, braving fierce winds, sheltering off the coast of Turkey and then Greece. But as they leave Crete, the ship is caught in a storm so dangerous that even crew members try to abandon the ship. To keep the vessel afloat, they have to throw out all their food grain. The ship is wrecked just as the shores of Malta come into view. The man and his fellow travelers swim ashore. In Malta, they wait months till they can find a ship to take them to Rome. Eventually the ship arrives in Syracuse. For two years, the man makes his case, talking to whoever will listen to him. But Rome has no use for his story, and eventually Paul the Apostle is arrested and beheaded by Emperor Nero's soldiers.

History is often like a carousel, in which the same movements take place again and again, with different protagonists. In Paul's time, the first century of the Common Era, it was the Roman Empire that controlled the roads and handed out permissions for travel. As a result, the Roman upper classes in the first two centuries of the Common Era are the first tourists of history. In the eighteenth century, it was the British who inaugurated modern tourism. Today, U.S. citizens are prolific travelers, thanks to a passport and a currency that opens most doors. Empires enable travel—both materially, by controlling roads and airways, and spiritually, by giving permits and permissions. And then the world rearranges itself to suit the empire's travelers. So prolific were the Romans in their recreational travels that the Greek writer Pausanias produced a Greece guidebook aimed at the

Romans. It is also during Roman times that the tradition of the Seven Wonders was established: the Hanging Gardens of Babylon, the Egyptian pyramids, the statue of Zeus, and other remarkable sights came to be imbued with that "must-see" quality that we are now so familiar with. And of course, the Romans complained. Here's Seneca's Tripadvisor review about the place where he stayed in Byzantium, modern-day Istanbul:

> I live right over a public bath. Just imagine every kind of human sound to make us hate our ears. When the muscular types work out and toss the lead weights, when they strain or make believe they are straining, I hear the grunting and many additional unpleasant sounds . . . Then there's the drink-seller with his various cries, the sausage-seller, the cake-seller, and all the managers of the restaurants, each hawking his wares with his own special intonation.

But what about those who didn't leave any written reviews or records? During the same period that the Roman Empire rose and fell, modern-day Eritrea and northern Ethiopia were the site of the ancient Kingdom of Aksum. It was one of the great kingdoms of antiquity, on par with ancient Persia or Rome. Strategically positioned at the crossroads of mercantile routes that connected the East African coast to the continent's interior, Aksumites traded with

Rome, Egypt, South Arabia, the Middle East, India, and China. We know very little about Aksum even though it developed a written script known as Ge'ez. The ruined palaces and tombs at Aksum, like many of the imperial ruins in the Global South, have not received even a tiny proportion of the reverence and scholarship and tourism that has attended Greek or Roman ruins, creating a nesting doll of missing histories.

And so as a child growing up in India, I tucked away the story of the queen of Sheba. The more I learned in school, the more improbable she felt. It wasn't simply her journey that felt improbable; it was her wisdom and courage and curiosity. At school we learned of how the Enlightenment brought the spirit of scientific inquiry to Europe and then the world, after long centuries in which so much of nothing happened that it was known as the Dark Ages. We memorized the sea route between India and Portugal, the way it curved around the Cape of Good Hope, before da Gama discovered us, our pepper and cinnamon. *Byhearting* was the verb we made up for committing to memory Wordsworth's "Daffodils" or Tennyson's "The Lotos-Eaters," which we recited in diction contests. After school, I hurried home to bolt down a late lunch, threw my yellow makkana around my head, and speed-walked to the tiled two-room madrassa next to our local mosque. Often I was late to class and slid quietly onto the last bench, joining my voice to the chorus of my classmates reciting the Fatiha. But one rainy day, Ra'uf ustad saw me trying to sneak in and asked why I was late.

"I stopped to eat lunch," I told him.

"Ah, lunch, very good, very good," he said, as he walked up and down between the rows. "What did you eat rice with?"

"With sambar and cabbage thoran," I said.

"But no pickle?" he asked. A frisson of energy went through the sleepy afternoon classroom. Where was this conversation going?

"Yes, there was pickle. Lemon pickle."

"Let me tell you a story about pickle," he said, sitting on the table at the front of the classroom after casting one eye upward to make sure he was not under a hole in the roof through which rain leaked in during monsoons.

"Once upon a time there was a king in this very Malayali land who saw a strange sight. He had just finished a delicious dinner and was eating his payasam when he looked up at the sky and saw the full moon split into two. The next day, he called his ministers and astrologers, but none of them knew what was going on," Ra'uf ustad began. "Any of you ever seen the moon split into two?"

"No!" we yelled obligingly. Gratefully, my classmates closed their notebooks and Qur'ans and unpropped the elbows on which drowsy heads were resting. We were no longer in a leaking madrassa; we were in the court of a long-ago Kerala king. The king, known as Cheraman Perumal, looked up at the skies every day and brooded. Had he imagined the moon cleaving? Luckily for him, a few days later, a small group of Arab merchants arrived in his court. The Perumal asked them about the cleaving of the moon. Respectfully they told him, this was a miracle performed by their prophet. "What is this prophet you speak of?" the Perumal asked. And they told him of a man called Muhammad in a city called Makka who spoke of one God. There were many who didn't believe him, and when they asked him to prove this one-God business, this soft-spoken man had prayed and then split the moon into two.

I must go see this Muhammad for myself, the Perumal decided. So when the monsoon winds started blowing west and the Arab merchants sailed back to their land, he went with them. Across the Arabian Sea he sailed and across the desert he took a caravan until he finally arrived in Makka and saw the prophet for himself, as the queen of Sheba had done centuries before in another city, with another prophet. And there in Makka, the Perumal became the first Muslim from the Indian subcontinent. There is no God but God, he said, and he decided that he would take this message back to India. "Okay, everyone, why are your Qur'ans closed? Open to Surah Al-Qamar and let us read what the Qur'an has to say about the moon getting split."

"But, ustad, I have a question," said Amina as she raised her hand.

"What is it?"

"What about the pickle?"

"Oh, yes, the pickle. We forgot about the pickle, didn't we? So when the Perumal arrived in Makka and met the prophet, he realized that he did not have any presents for him. Is that some way to go see a great prophet? The Perumal was ashamed of himself. He was, after all, the king of a great land. What would the prophet think of the people of Kerala? Then he remembered that he had some ginger pickle with him. You know how we pack pickles when we go on long journeys so that we will always have something to eat with rice? Even kings do that. So he took his pickle and gave it to the prophet. And the prophet accepted it graciously and shared it with his companions. Each one took a sliver of pickled ginger and ate it."

"What kind of pickles did they have in Arabia then?" Sayyid asked.

Ra'uf ustad paused to ponder the question while giggles rose in the class. Sitting on the back bench of the classroom, I could tell he was tempted by the question. He was a born storyteller, and it was always a battle between fact and plot. To tell what he knew or to embellish and embroider. I knew the pull myself. What stories he could tell of those foreign pickles he knew nothing about. The things they pickled in those lands. The djinns that loved those pickles.

"I don't know," he finally admitted.

Many of the stories I heard in my childhood fell through the cracks of record keeping. There was also a vagueness about where they began and where they ended. They began once upon a time and melted into larger story spirals unspooling away into the future. The Indian literary critic Ayyappa Paniker has written about the fundamentally different approach of Asian narratology in privileging the spatial over the temporal. While he is careful to offer the caveat that this is a generalization that comes with all the limitations of generalizations, Paniker notes that historic records in Asian cultures tend to locate events in a flexible

Shahnaz Habib

and elastic movement of time, while carefully assessing the geographic specificities of the story. As a result, he points out, "the shadow of a parable" looms over many Asian epics and folktales. Places are described in detail with attention to ecology and context, but since the stories are not moored in dates and times, they fail the history test. Compared to the history of the Western explorers who discovered India, with dates meticulously documented in history textbooks, the myths and stories of my childhood felt flimsy. The aura of holiness that surrounded some of these stories also lent itself to this vagueness. If a story came from the Qur'an or hadith or had some kind of religious connection, I learned not to ask too many questions. These stories were meant to be believed with eyes and ears closed. To ask where they came from or how they were told was to suggest that your faith was not waterproof. And so as these different frameworks collided against one another, the melting pot in my head broke into a thousand fragments, and I, like millions of other schoolchildren, learned to classify some stories as history and others as hearsay.

•

Sometime in the early 2000s, a few schoolchildren in a small town in Kerala called Pattanam, about twenty miles away from where I had grown up, were playing in a backyard when they started finding shards of pottery. Some of the shards caught the eye of a local schoolteacher, who got archaeologists involved. The clay used in some of the pottery was identified as volcanic soil, the kind found in the region of Mount Vesuvius. Archaeologists are now trying to pinpoint if this infraordinary town (Pattanam literally means *town*) could actually be Muziris, an ancient Indian harbor that is said to have been washed away during a medieval flood. When I visited the archaeological dig, there were mounds and mounds of pottery shards in a small house that was slowly transforming into a museum. Leaning on her shovel, an archaeologist told me that the pots were probably the amphorae in which the Romans kept olive oil during the long journey across the Mediterranean and the Arabian Sea.

Long before Columbus set out in search of Indian pepper, Muziris, a mysterious city on the western coast of India, was trading pepper with Rome. The Apicius, the most ancient European cookbook, calls for Malabar pepper in many of its recipes. Before it was swept away in the flood, Muziris was one of the linchpins of the maritime trading network that connected the Mediterranean, Indian, and Pacific Oceans. Operating entirely on seasonal monsoon winds, this network connected Rome to China by the beginning of the Common Era. The timing of monsoon winds meant that Muziris was conveniently located as a resting place on the navigation route, a place to shelter from the rains and repair ships till the winds switched directions. Naturally, Muziris became an emporium, where traders from different parts of the world met and poked at each other's wares. "Primum Emporium Indiae," Pliny the Elder called Muziris in his *Naturalis Historia*.

Muziris is fascinating of course, but I could not help wondering how I, growing up about forty-five minutes away from this ancient town, had never heard of it until now. I had spent the years of my childhood judging these small towns, rolling my eyes at their provincialness, fantasizing nonstop about escaping, and now the joke was on me. Merchants from Rome and Mesopotamia and China had stood on streets near me and bargained with one another. How is it possible to be so ignorant of one's own history? Growing up in Kerala, the artifacts of this muti-oceanic mercantile voyage were littered all over my childhood like clues. The kanji we drank in the mornings, the wok-shaped cheena chatti in which my parents cooked vegetables every day, the way Malabar Coast Muslims pronounce the third syllable of the word *Ramadan* with a soft velar *l* sound, an archaic pronunciation from medieval Arabic that has since been lost in the Arab world but persists in southern India. Despite this bread-crumb trail left behind by medieval travelers who arrived regularly on our shores, when we learned about explorers and navigators in school, we learned about Vasco da Gama and Columbus. Even now, having given myself this rickety homemade expertise in peeking under the rugs of travel history, I feel the gaps left by this autotopagnosia. To know one's history and geography is to know oneself.

There are at least two small towns in Kerala, sitting side by side, that vie for the title of Muziris. Pattanam is one of those towns. The other is nearby Kodungalloor, famous for its temple, which is dedicated to a fierce goddess. After visiting the freshly dug archaeological pits in Pattanam, my husband and I wandered around Kodungalloor, eating egg puffs and samosas at its many bakeries. Right off the main busy street stood a mosque reputed to have been built in the seventh century. It was a working mosque, and as we wandered around its premises, a bunch of schoolchildren filed out of the madrassa, giving us searching glances.

Legend has it that after Cheraman Perumal converted to Islam in Makka, he started his journey back to Kerala with one of the Prophet's companions, Malik bin Dinar, a young Persian man. But along the way, the Perumal fell sick and died and was buried in what is now Oman. Malik bin Dinar continued the journey, returning to Kerala to build a mosque and fulfill the Perumal's dream. If the legend is correct, he built the mosque in 629 CE, which would make it the third mosque to be built in the world, after the ones in Makka and Madina. Could this be that mosque? The mystery sat lightly on the mosque as we walked around quietly.

It is impossible to know for sure because the mosque has been rebuilt and renovated so many times that its architectural style is a syncretic mishmash. Most of its elements date back to at least the eleventh century. It is also possible that the mosque started its life as a Hindu or Buddhist temple before it was repurposed as a mosque, demolished by the Portuguese in the sixteenth century, and eventually rebuilt in a more modern style. Some of the oldest architectural elements such as lamps and wooden pillars seem to be borrowed from temple architecture. This mosque was a mosque before our notions of what a mosque should look like crystalized. It is a mosque full of maybes.

Years later, I heard about a long-lost Arabic text called Qissat Shakarwati Farmad, which had then just been translated into English. The title loosely translates as the story of Emperor Farmad. Farmad is none other than the Perumal, with the Malayalam consonants transformed into medieval Arabic. It details the story of an Indian king who witnesses the moon being split and dreams of Prophet Muhammad and travels with a group of Sufi pilgrims to Makka and accepts Islam and spends five years learning with the Prophet and marries a local woman and dies on the way back but his companions manage to reach Kerala and build the first mosque. There is no mention of pickles in this text, but when the prophet's companions ask him about Farmad, he tells them that he is a visitor from the land of pepper and ginger.

I think of this story, kept alive through legend and communal memory, every time I eat ginger pickle. I imagine how sailors and explorers throughout the history of travel must have carried pickles with them—they are a handy way to preserve meat and vegetables for long periods at sea or in deserts, and an even handier way to taste the flavors of home while far away. The pickle is the most convincing part of the legend for me. The ginger pickle is the moon split in half.

In the eighteenth century, Captain Cook would persuade his sailors to eat sauerkraut in order to combat scurvy while circumnavigating the world. As a result, Cook did not lose a single sailor. This was a breakthrough: it was common in the early days of European exploration to lose as much as half a ship's crew to scurvy.

But as far back as the fourth century, the travelogue of Faxian, a Buddhist scholar, mentions that Chinese sailors carried ginger to combat a disease that, from his description, sounds like scurvy. This is especially notable because vitamin C deficiency does not cause scurvy until after a full month of deprivation. In other words, those sailors were at sea for more than a month. Ibn Battuta, who visited China in the first half of the fourteenth century, described the junks he saw in one of its harbors: there were wooden tanks on board, on which sailors would cultivate ginger during their voyages. Crumbs of information such as these are crucial for remapping the history of naval exploration and freeing it from the European explorer-discoverer narrative.

At around the same time that the legend claims Malik bin Dinar was building the mosque in Kodungalloor, the Chinese monk Xuanzang was traveling to India. He was one of thousands of Chinese pilgrims who traveled to the Buddhist holy places in India, most of them taking the Silk Road through Central Asia and then returning via maritime routes through Southeast Asia. According to Stephen Gosch and Peter Stearns, authors of *Premodern Travel in World History*, the Buddhist monks from China are among the most adventurous long-distance travelers of the first millennium CE. Many of them were scholar-monks, and they were not just paying respects to the Buddha; they were learning Sanskrit and collecting Buddhist texts for translation into Chinese.

By the time Xuanzang was ordained as a monk at the age of twenty, most of these texts had been translated, but in a move that will be familiar to overachieving students everywhere, he decided to consult the primary sources in order to avoid any mistakes that might have crept into the translations. So he crossed the mountains into India, visited the Bodhi tree under which the Buddha achieved enlightenment, and then traveled to Nalanda, the ancient Indian university, where he was welcomed warmly. He stayed in that immense complex of lecture halls and monasteries and libraries for sixteen years before taking the scenic route back to China.

Thus, contrary to the notion of the Dark Ages, the medieval era is rich with travel. Caravans full of gold and salt were moving through Western Africa. Polynesians were sailing the Pacific, establishing a vast confederacy of island kingdoms that traded with one another. And in Asia, the Arab merchant, the Chinese sailor, and the Buddhist scholar had managed to link six thousand miles, stretching from Basra to Guangzhou. By the early ninth century, Arab and Chinese ships were regularly sailing between these two harbors. Arab traders controlled the global supply chain of spices, textiles, and other "Eastern" commodities from China and India, moving them through Middle Eastern cities like Aleppo and Cairo before continuing to Venice and elsewhere in Europe. Many Arab merchants were also slave traders, who traveled from the Persian Gulf down the coast as far as what we know today as Mozambique or moved between the kingdoms of West Africa and the North African coast.

The Muslim and Chinese empires and the trading routes

they established set the stage for one of history's most famous travelers: Marco Polo. One might think that the
man credited with being the first European to reach China
would be an ambitious explorer, with a plan and a map. In
fact, Marco Polo was an adolescent who went on a trip with
his father and uncle. Years after he returned to Europe, he
narrated the story of his travels to a fellow prisoner, who
wrote it up for posterity. It is extremely possible that this
ghostwriter may have taken several liberties with Polo's
story. Historians speculate that the stories of Christian miracles and the mythical animals of the East were products of
the ghostwriter's fertile imagination. It is also possible that
Marco Polo's travelogue was significantly altered by the nu-
merous scribes who copied it afterward.

Having said all that, we do know that Marco Polo was
born in Venice in 1254, into a family of merchants who
specialized in the maritime commerce between Venice
and Constantinople. His father and uncle returned from a
trading trip east with a remarkable story about meeting the
Kublai Khan, who gave them a passport-like document to
travel through his territories and beyond. Upon their return
to Venice, they were eager to go back east and make their
way to China, this time taking adolescent Marco with them.
They sailed to Jerusalem, after which most of the rest of their
journey was by land, possibly through the Anatolian heartland and then up the Persian plateau. Narrowly escaping
highway brigands and taking advantage of the caravanserai
network established by Muslim kings and left mostly intact
by the Mongols, they rode through Central Asia, crossing

mountain ranges and deserts, finally crossing into western China in 1273. In Kublai Khan's employ, Polo traveled to far-flung provinces and reported back to the Khan. The China we glimpse through Marco Polo's eyes is a China of mansions and bridges and pleasure boats and hotels and paper money made from the bark of mulberry trees.

Marco Polo is colloquially considered the first European to reach China. Historians usually hasten to add that this may not be true: It is possible that Europeans arrived in China as early as the classical period. Polo was merely the first to leave a record. But if we set aside the question of whether or not Marco Polo was the first European to reach China, there is a more interesting question: Why is it an achievement to be the first European to reach China? Who is that an achievement for? We rarely hear about the first Asian to reach Europe or the first African to reach the Americas. But the first European to reach China and the first European to reach India by sea and the first European to reach the Americas? Their names are household names, not because this is a major achievement, but because of the European investment in the idea of the first European to reach these "other" places.

This is why we hear so much about someone like Marco Polo, who happened to be in the right place at the right time for European writers to seize on his chronicles of being a European abroad, but we hear so little about the delegation of thirty Africans who traveled through Spain, France, and Rome in 1306, six years after Marco Polo's travel stories were published. They were sent by the Ethiopian king Wedem Ar'ad, who was hoping to create a pan-Christian alliance to stem the growing infiltration of Muslim rulers into his continent. This delegation of Orthodox Christian Ethiopians called on rulers in Spain, visited Pope Clement V in France, and then paid their respects at the churches of Saints Peter and Paul in Rome, eventually sailing home from Genoa. In the next few centuries, the Ethiopian kings consolidated their power, built a remarkable network of churches, established an alliance of protection with the Coptic Church in Egypt, and shored up an Orthodox Christian bulwark against the Muslim empire. Their monks and diplomats would travel to Europe often, in search of Christian relics and artisans to bring home to what they considered the headquarters of the Christian Church.

Their obscurity is especially remarkable considering that Europe, at this time, was already trading in Black bodies—the thirty travelers of 1306 who came of their own volition and agency, representing their powerful African Christian emperor, clearly considered themselves to be on equal footing with the Europeans. If the Industrial Revolution had started in Khartoum or Addis and if African countries had become colonial powers ruling over Europe, doubtless we would have history books about how they discovered Europe.

Instead, what do we have? Here's Edward Gibbon, the author of *The History of the Decline and Fall of the Roman Empire*, writing about the culturally rich and transnationally active world of medieval Ethiopia: "Encompassed on all sides by the enemies of their religion, the Aethiopians slept near a thousand years, forgetful of the world, by whom they were forgotten. They were awakened by the Portuguese, who, turning the southern promontory of Africa, appeared in India and the Red Sea, as if they had descended through the air from a distant planet."

The Portuguese are also often credited for waking up India. On May 21, 1492, the Portuguese navigator Vasco da Gama arrived on the shore of Kerala after a long and tortuous journey via the Atlantic Ocean. Five months later, Christopher Columbus would make landfall in what is now the Bahamas and proudly declare that he had found India. So at least da Gama can be credited with having arrived in the right place. In fact, he had stopped in the port of Malindi, in modern Kenya, to pick up an Indian sailor who helped him navigate to the South Indian coast. Da Gama's ship was part of the spice race, which, as Amitav Ghosh writes in *The Nutmeg's Curse*, was the space race of its time.

Certainly it was a dramatic moment for da Gama and the Portuguese empire and Europe. But the Malabar coast was used to arrivals and departures. In fact, according to the anonymous author of the *Roteiro*, translated as *A Journal of the First Voyage of Vasco da Gama 1497–1499*, when the ship arrived at Kozhikode, da Gama sent a convict ashore to find out more. The first European to step on an Indian shore was the convict Joao Nunez. He was greeted by two Tunisian merchants, who welcomed him warmly, speaking in Castilian and Genoese: "The Devil take you! What brought you here?"

•

Having been spoon-fed all the pabulum about Western colonial powers waking up Asian and African countries, nothing quite prepared me for my first sight of Lalibela, the rock churches in northern Ethiopia. My friend and I arrived there during the pilgrimage season of January 2019, when the Orthodox Church was celebrating Christmas. The eleven underground churches of Lalibela, built in the twelfth century, are Ethiopian Christianity's greatest monuments.

All of them are monolithic, each carved out of a single massive block of red volcanic rock. Connected to one another by underground paths, most of which are now closed off for safety, Lalibela is a vast complex of rock-hewn cathedrals, monasteries, and tombs. Legend has it that after visiting Jerusalem, King Lalibela had this complex built as a faithful homage. Our guide told us the king wanted his people to have an Orthodox Jerusalem so they could be spared the arduous travel to Palestine. Or maybe, like kings everywhere, he wanted to build something big, something that would keep his name alive for centuries.

For two days, we walked around the churches, in a daze of wonder and awe, alongside the thousands of pilgrims who crowded into these mystical underground spaces with us. We hadn't planned on being there during the Ethiopian Christmas. Pearl and I, traveling from my North American winter and her Australian summer, had chosen the first week of January to travel together because it was one of the only times in the year that our holidays from work coincided. It was also a convenient time to leave our children in the care of our spouses. Knowing that we would be visiting Lalibela during the Ethiopian Christmas, we imagined a busy time. Nothing prepared us. As our taxi climbed the hill up to town, we saw hundreds of pilgrims, dressed in white, many of them barefoot, walking up the hill. The driver of our taxi pointed to the buckets of water at intervals along the road. For many locals, it is an honor to wash pilgrims' feet, he said.

That night, the sleepy town we had arrived in transformed: thousands of pilgrims set up tents and cooked over campfires on the streets of Lalibela. A pilgrim market sprang into life, selling rosaries and shawls and monk's robes and goatskin portraits of saints. Over the course of the next few days, our paltry tourist itinerary intersected with this magnificent influx of pilgrims from around Ethiopia and beyond.

Lalibela's churches are marvels of subterranean engineering. Some of them are freestanding, while others are carved into the volcanic basalt. This was church before our notions of what a church should look like crystalized. One of the churches, Bete Giyorgis (House of Saint George), is shaped like a cross, like many European cathedrals. Except that since our first view of Bete Giyorgis is looking down on it, as a bird would see it, the huge cross looks as if it is embedded into the ground. It is an invitation to kneel and kiss the earth, fulfilled magnificently in architecture.

King Lalibela wanted his homage to Jerusalem to be perfect in every way, so the churches contain replicas of Christ's tomb, the Ark of the Covenant, and other potent symbols. There is a waterway called Yordannos running through the complex to symbolize the river Jordan. Even the tunnels connecting the churches are symbolic—the early Christians of Jerusalem used tunnels to go to church in secret. So the king insisted that the rock churches too should be connected by an elaborate system of tunnels. Murals line many of the walls of the underground churches. In the darkness of this subterranean world, the angels and saints in the murals merged with the shadows and silhouettes of living, breathing humans, as if we were all part of one grand story.

Sometimes that story was all too human. In each church, the line of pilgrims would wend its way to a priest sitting near the altar and he would offer the cross for kissing. A kiss at the top of the cross, a kiss at the bottom, a touch of the cross to the forehead. Hundreds of kisses every hour. Some of the priests looked bored and long-suffering. I have seen that look before, I thought to myself, and then in a crowded church where pilgrims who had been fasting all day were sitting on the floor waiting for Mass to begin, I remembered. The glazed eyes of the priests reminded me of station managers in New York subway stations handing out transfer tickets on the days when the train is not working. It didn't matter. The pilgrim does not go on a pilgrimage to have a special moment with the priest. In fact, the ritualism of the moment was exactly the point. To lose oneself in a crowd. To walk the beaten path. To wait and to be bored. Perhaps what separates the tourist from the pilgrim is not the reasons for their travel but the satisfaction that the pilgrim finds in what frustrates the tourist.

After my friend and I visited Lalibela, we hired a driver to drive us several hours west, to the town of Bahir Dar. We drove through red canyons and plateaus blistered by the sun, on roads of bone-crushing roughness, eventually arriving in the much greener Nile valley.

In one of the little towns we drove through, our driver, Wondessa, stopped near a shack and ran out to buy a bundle of leaves. He chewed on them for the rest of the trip, facing off with dust-covered long-distance buses and yelling at schoolchildren along the way, pausing abruptly to donate money and kiss crosses at roadside altars. "This is chat," he said when I asked him about the leaves. "It gives me strength." Chat, a mild stimulant, is legal and immensely popular in Ethiopia. Certainly it seemed to improve Wondessa's mood as he dropped us off on the shore of the Blue Nile, so that we could ferry across to a cabin site overlooking the Blue Nile Falls.

Perched almost on the shoulder of the waterfall, the cabin site, which is a collection of huts and tents, sits next to the river as it gathers force rushing toward the falls. The Blue Nile Falls is early in the course of the Nile River, before it flows into Sudan and meets the White Nile (which originates in Uganda).

"It used to be better," I was told when I gushed about the 360 degrees of sky and water and birds and trees and stone that met my eye from our tent. Bele, one of the guides who worked at the cabin site, shook his head despondently and told me about a dam upstream that had been altering the flow of the river. "Fifteen years ago, all this used to be river," he told me, indicating the cliff on which we were sitting. The river had been shriveling, as the planet overheated. He pointed to the banks on the other side where some children were playing ball. "That is where we would bring cows to drink water."

"They are no good," he told me a few minutes later when I admired the footwork of one of those kids as he nimbly jumped from rock to rock to catch an errant ball. "The Ethiopian football team is very bad," he added sadly.

In Bele, I recognized a fellow grumpy. In his general glumness about the world, I recognized my own natural instinct to expect the worst. People are terrible and the world is an absolutely miserable place. This baseline skepticism means that grumpies are useful at history. They rarely have illusions about human motivations. So of course, when I said something about how everyone we met seemed excited about the new Ethiopian prime minister, Bele sat down to explain to me all the tensions simmering under the current moment of hope. Yes, the new prime minister, Abiy Ahmed, had promised far-reaching reforms, yes, the peace with Eritrea, yes, there were women in the cabinet, but also— decades upon decades of distrust. The ethnic tensions had not gone anywhere; they were waiting underneath, gathering force. The previous government had enriched itself and its own ethnic group. Their spies were everywhere, and they still occupied all the important positions, he told me. Bele was in no mood to forgive the rich kleptocracy that had managed to grab all the foreign aid. When he was younger, Bele went to Sudan to work. The government there was much more proactive compared to the one in Ethiopia, he said, gesturing with his hands as if to indicate all the missing hospitals and schools and bridges.

Less than two years later, I remembered Bele and the toughness of his pessimism when civil war broke out in northern Ethiopia. Lalibela itself would become the site of multiple battles between government-allied forces and rebels, and prime minister Abiy Ahmed, who was awarded the Nobel Peace Prize in 2019, would preside over a gruesome military offensive against the northern state of Tigray, killing many thousands of Ethiopians. At the moment, there is no agreement as to exactly how many thousands.

"It is not easy to change things," Bele told me sadly in 2019. "Look, this is the problem," he said suddenly, pointing to a cluster of chat bushes near my tent. The oval leaves grew abundantly around the river. Ethiopia should have been cultivating food; instead, there was too much chat, and too many people sat around and chewed chat, Bele told me. "I hate it. It ruined my generation, and now it is ruining the young ones." He was hoping the new prime minister would ban the stimulant.

Abal, who owned the cabin site, rolled his eyes when he overheard all this. "Chat is good stuff," he told me, and, gesturing at the book I was holding, he said, "You will be able to read three books in the same time." The young Ethiopians who were using chat needed it to stay on top of their studies, according to Abal. He shuddered when he thought of how they suffered. Universities were cruel places that made you read books and take exams. And the dam upriver was going to create jobs, improve water supply, increase Ethiopia's standing in Africa (show Sudan a thing or two), and bring more tourists, he told me.

"How will it help tourism?" I asked him.

"See that waterfall?" He pointed to the one right next to the cabin site. "Every Saturday at eleven, when the tour buses bring the white people, the local government opens the dam. So there is more water in this waterfall then. Like, four times as much. And the white people feel like they have seen something great. Blue Nile! Africa! Wow! They take photos for fifteen minutes, and when the buses leave at eleven thirty, we close the dam and everything goes back to normal." He laughed. "Sometimes if my guests are very, very good and they are going to leave before eleven, I call up my friend who works in the powerhouse and ask him to turn the dam on."

At lunch the next day, two charming German backpackers who were traveling around Ethiopia for a few months shuddered when I told them I was from Brooklyn. Please no more, they begged; Leipzig had now become Hypezig thanks to all the Brooklynites moving to Germany in search of health insurance and cheap rent. Next week when I got back to Brooklyn, I'd start physically blocking people from moving to Berlin, I promised them.

Stefan is shocked to hear that I would be back in Brooklyn so soon. "That is so short time to fly all this way." He smirked. They were both backpacking in East Africa for three months. "And maybe after, we don't know yet."

I felt a protective pang for the measly two weeks that I had carved out between childcare and work. My friend Pearl was texting her children in Sydney as we spoke. When we were adolescents in India, staying in a hostel with a 7:00 p.m. curfew, we would lie in bed fantasizing about all the places we would travel to. We would try out place names to feel them on our tongues: Singapore, Kilimanjaro, Valparaiso. Money, we knew, would always be in short supply. But we had no idea that time was not a bottomless ocean. Our time had finally come, and there was so little of it.

I wanted to tell Stefan how much more precious our travel was because there was so little of it while also saying something deep and cutting about how it must be nice to be young and male and European and spend months bumming around a Third World country while resenting those who wanted to move to his city in Germany, but also, and this might have seemed irrelevant but it was not, did he know that the queen of Sheba was probably the first traveler in world history, and I wanted to say all this in six or seven words so that it could feel like a punch line, boom, something he would forever remember with gratitude even as he curled in shame and died. But I also wanted to shake Stefan by the shoulders and tell him: Keep going. Turn those three months into six months, a year, do it now before the ocean of time shrivels into a tiny bathtub. Because if you are lucky, your time, too, will become precious.

But his eyes were glazing over and maybe mine were too—by now, somehow we were chewing chat, or "Ethiopian green salad" as Abal called it. Lunch had given way to a coffee ceremony as his friends dropped in, each carrying his or her bundle of chat. As Abal passed around thimble-sized cups of rich black coffee, he gave each of us, his guests, a little bundle of chat. "It's your first time," he said. "Next time won't be free."

Abal and his friends reminded one another about the backpacker from the year before who got a bit too fond of chat. "Can't I just stay here for the rest of my life, eating injera and chewing chat and drinking coffee?" he'd asked Abal. They imitated his glassy eyes and his slow drawl.

"Be careful, or this will happen to you; that's why the first one is free," one of Abal's friends told us. He took pity on us and showed us how to chew chat slowly and judiciously by wedging a small stack of leaves into the side of a cheek and chewing on it bit by bit, releasing the bitter juices while also chewing some peanuts to blunt the bitterness.

"If I start talking of how amazing this place is and how we could just stay here for the rest of our lives, drag me out of here and put me on the plane home," I told Pearl.

"Same for me." She nodded.

Somebody put on music. More friends dropped in. Every now and then, a beloved song came on and all the Ethiopians in the tent sang along and swayed. The tent itself was swaying, and the floor seemed to be moving languorously. Even Bele was chewing away, so I asked him about his anti-chat principles. "I have a sinus problem today. This will help open my nostrils," he informed me coldly.

Yet another German backpacker arrived and took off the most enormous backpack I had seen. He had met Abal's brother in town on his way to the cabin site and the brother had sent Christmas money to Abal, so he could give it to their mother, so she could buy a rooster for their Christmas feast. Six hundred birr in crumpled notes. I remembered my uncles then, so many of them working in Qatar or Saudi Arabia or Dubai during my childhood, sending home money through a friend of a friend of a friend who was coming to Kerala for his annual visit.

It was interesting, this familiarity I felt toward Ethiopia. The guidebooks suggested a place foreign and remote, a proud people, grand monuments in a state of sad decay. But instead of the promised exotic frisson, I felt the kinship of a fellow Third World country. The little towns that operated like hucksters, the way history sat on skin like an itchy scar that must not be scratched, the obsession with dams. And of course, there were many Indians in Addis, many of them working in schools and hospitals.

But even beyond this—and now the floor was certainly dancing—there seemed to be some long-lost genetic connection. The man I saw on the ferry who looked like he could be from a village in Kerala but turned out to be Ethiopian. The woman on the plane who asked me in Amharic for my phone charger and, when I didn't understand, upbraided me for not speaking my mother tongue. The shape of that nose; the expression in this pair of eyes.

There has been a small community of East Africans in South Asia since medieval times. The Siddis, as they are known, arrived as merchants and sailors. Many of them are also the descendants of enslaved people—the Arab and the Portuguese slave trade brought thousands of Black people from the hinterlands of the Swahili coast to the South Asian subcontinent. But the Siddis are a distinctive community, and supposedly there has been little racial mixing between them and the South Asian population. With very little to go on except a gut feeling, I wondered if the mixing of peoples is much more widespread than we realize. "What do you think?" I nudged Pearl. "Wouldn't these faces fit right into Kerala?"

"It's like those Bollywood movies, where long-lost brothers find each other when they accidentally see each other's birthmarks," she replied.

"Yes, exactly!" I was so pleased she got it. How lovely it was to come up with a little theory and then have it scientifically confirmed so quickly. I felt such an upsurge of affection for Pearl, for this brilliant idea we had to travel together, for the girls we were and the old women we would become.

"Isn't this the bestest coffee you have ever had?" she asked.

"It is. You know, we could just stay here, couldn't we? For the rest of our lives?"

"Absolutely. We will regret it if we leave, alle," she replied.

•

Against the vacuum created by Europe's fascination with its own hero's journey, one medieval man stands out: Ibn Battuta, beloved of travel historians everywhere. As a young man in Tangier in North Africa, a frontier town of the fourteenth century, Ibn Battuta had set out on a pilgrimage at the age of twenty-one. One might wonder if this was not a very tender age for a pilgrimage. But, according to Ross E. Dunn, author of *The Adventures of Ibn Battuta: A Muslim Traveler of the 14th Century*, the hajj in Ibn Battuta's time was almost always more than a journey to Makka and home again. Rather, it was a rihla, a grand study tour of the great mosques and madrassas of the Islamic heartland, an opportunity to acquire books and diplomas, deepen one's knowledge of theology and law, and commune with refined and civilized men. Thus the hajj in that era was more akin to the Grand Tour that European aristocrats undertook in the seventeenth and eighteenth centuries than to the ten-day pilgrimage that we know today. It was also a ritual migration, often involving a caravan moving through the steppes of northern Africa toward Makka, collecting thousands of pilgrims on its way like a rolling snowball. Many pilgrims might have had other aims—trade or study or diplomacy—but the hajj was the overriding theme.

Looking at Ibn Battuta's career as a traveler, I wonder if he was propelled at least as much by a quest for adventure as any spiritual desire. It was not unheard of for a hajj journey to take two or even three years in those days, but Ibn Battuta would take twenty-four years to return home. He would marry six women along the way; visit Alexandria, Cairo, and Damascus; and, after performing hajj, instead of setting off home to Morocco, he would take off toward Basra and Isfahan and Baghdad.

Wouldn't you? Imagine being footloose and twenty-one years old and tasting the world on a platter and knowing that you can do so much better than going back to dusty little Tangier where the same old lawyer job your father and his father had done for decades is waiting for you. Instead you could be a medieval Muslim cosmopolite, caravanning off to different destinations, confident of finding hospitality and employment in any of the many newly established centers of Islamic civilization in the farther regions of Asia and Africa. The hajj brought home to Ibn Battuta that he was not just a Moroccan lawyer; he was a citizen of Dar al-Islam, the geographic and cultural span of the Islamic world. Just as Marco Polo had the good fortune of belonging to a Venetian mercantile family, Ibn Battuta lived at a time when people like him moved through the world freely and prosperously. Why would you go home?

I moved to the United States at the age of twenty-four for graduate school. My "statements of purpose" and scholarship essays were full of high-minded ideas about media and culture and education. But the truth is, I just wanted to see the world. It was all I dreamed of: being elsewhere, moving through anonymous crowds, seeing things I had only read about, being far away from the things I knew. I had no place in mind; any place would do. What were the chances for an Indian woman like me, my passport bearing the stigma of the Third World, traveling the world? An international education was my pretext, and how well it worked. Just as Ibn Battuta possibly acted more religious than he was, I pretended to be more ambitious than I was. Just as he joined the caravan of pilgrims and merchants on their way to Makka, I joined the annual caravan of international students floating toward the East Coast of the United States. I came to New York, not because I wanted to be here specifically but because it was not home. Here was a place someone would give me money to be in. Across the seven centuries separating us, I can easily sympathize with Ibn Battuta as he finishes his third hajj in Makka and, still feeling restless, sets his eye on India, the court of Muhammad bin Tughlak, the wealthiest Muslim king of the time.

The rihla of Ibn Battuta has no specific destination. At each place he arrives, Ibn Battuta figures out where to go next. He has very little loyalty, turning against previous patrons when it suits him. He is not trying to win any prizes for his country or discover new lands; he is just a Moor unmoored. So, though he is often compared to the explorers who became famous in the Age of Exploration (Columbus and da Gama and Vespucci et al.), his journey is quite different from their ambitious voyages. Ibn Battuta is a vaynokki of the world.

It was on a diplomatic mission for Tughlak that Battuta arrived in Kerala. On the Malabar coast, he survived a shipwreck and a near-drowning. The adventures of Ibn Battuta in Kerala, but also pretty much everywhere on his travels, are a litany of troubles. He survives brigands, kidnappings, wars, shipwrecks, pirates, starvation, and disease. He stares death in the face so many times in his narrative that I lost count when I read it. And he is not a brave man! His rihla is full of honest detail about trembling with fear, begging for mercy, getting ready to meet his Maker, and then somehow surviving yet another danger, in some cases almost comically. At one point, he writes, the men who were directed to kill him forgot to, alhamdulillah, onward and upward.

This was the standard lot of the medieval traveler— danger, that is, not the escapes. Famously, the word *travel* is etymologically related to *travail*, which in turn has its origins in the Latin noun *trapezium*—a three-pronged metal device that ancient Romans used to torture prisoners. Today, for us, travel is a reprieve from the travails of work and daily life. But in those early days, travel was fraught with travail. Medieval roadways were infested with brigands while pirate ships trolled the high seas. In *The Medieval Invention of Travel*, Sharon Legassie points out that "in the Middle Ages, travel was nasty, brutish and long." When setting out on a pilgrimage or a trading journey, medieval travelers could look forward to weeks and months of slow and life-threatening travel, which often meant that they were effectively severing domestic ties for the duration of their journeys. By the time Ibn Battuta returned home, his infant son and his parents were dead.

•

I missed my own little family intensely throughout the two weeks I spent away from them. Whenever I saw families, I felt a pang. In every market, I looked for souvenirs for my husband and daughter. I woke up in the middle of the night so I could call them and hear them chatter about art class and composting and how annoying the subway was being. Longing for the people I loved lay close to my skin like a thermal layer, generating its own heat. Right on top of that was frustration—why couldn't I just enjoy my measly two weeks without feeling this pointless homesickness?

On my last day near the Blue Nile, I went out for an early walk. By circling the cliff, I could get to the front of the waterfall. Bele had loaned me his trusty bamboo walking stick, and I used it to pick my way up and down the muddy riverbank. Already I could picture how different it would be in a few years or decades: the ticket booths, the vendors, all the paraphernalia of development and the overflowing garbage bins in its wake. I thought of the women I had seen ten minutes ago, a long line of them, carrying pots or dragging livestock, walking miles and miles to the weekend market across the river. So many of them would find much easier work in the tourism industry. There would be a chain hotel where the cabin site was now. And the people of this village would become that strange stratum of modern society that is known as "locals." So much gained, so much more lost.

But who was I to judge the tourists who had not yet arrived? The riverbank was a slippery slope and I picked my way carefully. I had booked the cabin site online, traveled here in a comfortable car, paid dollars for bottled water, and now here I was pretending that I was a traveler, not a tourist. It's insidious, this desire to set one's own tourism story apart from that of other tourists.

Before I could begin a proper guilt trip, I found my way to a flat dry rock in front of the waterfall, and sat on it. It would be hours before the tour bus came, so the falls were at a quarter of their potential. I considered taking a photo, but just couldn't be bothered. Who needs one more waterfall photo? Especially that of one-fourth of a waterfall. Instead, I watched the white water plummet into the green river before it flowed down to Sudan and Egypt all the way to the Mediterranean Sea.

I noticed the birds then. A bunch of birds were flying into the waterfall and out of it and into the waterfall and out of it. They were too far away for me to make out colors, but I could tell that they were a few different kinds. Big birds and small birds, birds with incredible wingspans and tiny birds that kept fluttering against the blue sky as if they were barely staying afloat. I sat there watching them, trying to decipher them. What were they doing? Were they drinking water? Were they bathing? Were they hunting one another? It was such a silly way to get anything done—flying in and out of a waterfall. Did everything have to be a stupid mystery today? And just as I had this ridiculous thought, I understood—oh, they were playing.

Of course they were playing. The fun of it made me smile. Imagine what a daredevil racecourse the waterfall must be if you are a bird. What a pleasure it must be to feel the water pour over your tiny body. What a joy to test its power and weight against your tiny bird bones. I had always thought of curiosity as a human impulse, but it was, in fact, an animal impulse. We inherited it from the birds, this need to see for oneself what the world was like. What an ancient thrill to be inside a tiny body feeling the cold, the wetness, the heaviness, the light, Jerusalem, Makka, Lalibela. And for about half a moment, the world was water and I was a bird.

Chapter

SIX

✈

I HAVE SO MANY PHOTOS OF IT. BOUGAINVILLEA DRAPING over walls next to cobbled streets, bougainvillea running wild over the iron railings of restaurants, bougainvillea bonsai in a rock garden. They are hardy, flowering even in near-droughts. They come in an array of lollipop colors, from golden yellow to magenta. They fit into any context, somehow managing to look as if they have always belonged here. Cobbled street in Rome? Sure. Beachside balcony in Miami? Why not. Dusty Delhi road? No problem.

I remember my mental muscles twitching the first time I learned that the papery petals of the bougainvillea are actually not flowers; they are leaves. We lived then in a small house, rented from a family friend. The neighbors on both sides were wealthy and their houses had gardens, and the households had stay-at-home mothers and servants to water the plants. As a result, a luxuriant bough of bougainvillea clambered over one tall wall and spilled over into the yard between our house and their wall. I thought of it as our bougainvillea and felt even then the grace of this plant, climbing over walls, bridging social chasms, bringing its beauty to people who had done nothing to deserve it.

It was my aunt, an agricultural scientist, who told me that the bougainvillea flowers were not flowers. The scientific term is *bract*—a modified leaf. Bougainvillea bracts come in extraordinary colors, from shades of pink that go from the lightest of blushes to extravagant fuchsias. There are crinkly yellows that remind me of crumpled first drafts and oranges and saffrons and whites, often brilliant against the lush green leafery that surrounds them. "These bracts are actually protecting the real flowers, by pretending to be flowers," my aunt told me, teasing out the tiny white flower hiding inside a cluster of magenta bracts.

My parents eventually built a house of their own. By the time they finished the house, we children had left home. After years of living in a house that was too small, my parents now live alone in a house that is too big for them. My mother, whose bank-clerk salary was the only source of income for most of our childhood, started gardening, turning her practical maternal attention to green peppers and curry leaves and aloe vera. "I am not interested in flowers," she would say, frugally choosing "useful plants" to make the most of her small yard. But then the bougainvillea bug bit her. One year when I came home from Brooklyn, there was a row of pots on the wall, with bougainvilleas in different colors spilling out of them. It was my job that summer to water them carefully. Bougainvillea roots are weak—they are climbers, so they have no idea how to support their own weight. What they have instead is a strong grip—using their thorns, they wind their way up or down, finding a home for themselves on hedges, walls, other trees, making themselves both ordinary and spectacular at the same time. They reminded me of the way I, too, was clawing my way up the walls of another country, while my roots shallowed in the ground.

And so I started reading about them. Bougainvilleas are named after the eighteenth-century French admiral Louis Antoine de Bougainville, who led a voyage of circumnavigation around the world. His expedition was part of the race between the British and the French to make new discoveries in the South Pacific. Bougainville's expedition was the first one to include a government-sponsored naturalist on board, Philibert Commerçon.

The expedition arrived in Rio de Janeiro in 1767, where Commerçon noticed trees with bright mauve and magenta bracts. He named this new genus Bougainvillea, in honor of the expedition leader. Commerçon is said to have collected at least five specimens of this then-unusual plant in Rio de Janeiro—today these specimens can be seen in various herbariums in France.

But was it really Commerçon who noticed these plants first? Commerçon was not a man in robust health; he would go on to die in Madagascar during the same expedition. On board, he was accompanied by an assistant who also happened to be an expert botanist. There is some speculation that this assistant was his lover, a woman who had disguised herself as a man to fit into the masculine atmosphere of the ship. According to Glynis Ridley's *The Discovery of Jeanne Baret: A Story of Science, the High Seas, and the First Woman to Circumnavigate the Globe*, it was Baret who first noticed and described this plant—and perhaps most of the 6,000-odd natural specimens that the expedition collected, many of these named for Commerçon or Bougainville. In Ridley's telling, Baret went looking for medicinal plants in the forests of Rio de Janeiro because Commerçon was sick, and she was drawn to the red bracts of the bougainvillea because of the doctrine of signatures, according to which the shapes and colors of plants can reveal their uses.

The very next year, Captain Cook and his *Endeavour* expedition would arrive in Rio de Janeiro. Joseph Banks, the naturalist on board, and his team were not allowed to disembark by the Portuguese rulers, but according to their diaries, they managed to outwit the sentinels and sneak out at night by boat. The *Endeavour* returned to London with various plant specimens and the first recorded sketch of a bougainvillea—a finished watercolor that is now in the collection of the Natural History Museum of London.

And thus the bougainvillea was discovered and described and identified. But of course, it was neither Commerçon nor Baret who discovered the bougainvillea. The flower is native to the places we now know as Brazil, Argentina, and Peru.

People of color often use air quotes when we talk of explorers who "discovered" the Americas or India or various Pacific islands. Alas, it is hard to translate air quotes to text. Even when retranslated back as quote marks (see "discovered"), something is missing. My fingers often itch to include the eye-rolling and smirking that we use to accompany air quotes. I propose instead a new word: *pseudiscovery.* The silent *p*, I hope, will convey the silence of our air quotes, the people and places who were rendered invisible when Europeans pseudiscovered them.

Today the bougainvillea is the cliché flower you expect to see in cute colonial towns. It is known as Santa Rita in Uruguay, trinitaria in Mexico, jahanamiya in some Arab countries, bunga kertas in Indonesia. I love also all the vernacular variations of *bougainvillea*, the pronunciations catching the local accents—from *bowgainvilla* in my own Malayalam to *bumbagilia* in Spanish. But before the bougainvillea was pseudiscovered and grown in the herbariums of France and propagated in the gardens of England, before it was transplanted into tropical colonies around the world by the British, French, and Portuguese, before it acquired all these different names, it must have had a name. What was the bougainvillea called in Tupi or Guarani or any of the three thousand Indigenous languages that were spoken in Brazil before the colonizers arrived? It must have been called something else. Or rather, it was something else. In other words, the bougainvillea is not a bougainvillea just as its flower is not a flower.

•

In *Braiding Sweetgrass*, Robin Wall Kimmerer writes about coming across the word *puhpowee*, the Anishinabe word for the force that causes mushrooms to push up from the earth overnight. "As a biologist I was stunned that such a word existed," Kimmerer writes, adding that Western natural science has no such term, no words to hold the mystery of invisible energies. While she admires botany for its "inti-mate vocabulary that names each little part" of a plant, she is conscious that something is missing when you reduce a creature to its working parts. Kimmerer calls this "a grave loss in translation from the native languages."

When those seafaring French naturalists aboard the *Étoile* decided to call this delicate pink flower a bougain-villea and when the "Buginvillea spectabilis" was finally entered into the second volume of the fourth edition of Linnaeus's *Species Plantarum* in 1799, what was lost was not just the local name of a bract. It was one of countless missed opportunities to counterpoint the Enlightenment view of the world, which European explorers carried around the world as the foundation of knowledge. Perhaps there was a brief moment there when we could have charted a differ-ent relationship to nature that might have saved our planet from the environmental blunders that were set in motion with the Industrial Revolution.

It is also worth remembering that the male European dominance over natural history in this particular mo-ment represented a break in another tradition: herbalism. Traditionally, across many cultures, women were the mis-tresses of the world of herbs and plants. Natural history was mostly a domestic science, used in medicine and cooking. Jeanne Baret's biographer, Glynis Ridley, speculates that Baret was an herb woman who came into contact with the naturalist Commerçon because she was a source of infor-mation for him. But as flora and fauna specimens from Asia and Africa and South America started flowing into Europe through explorations, investors and governments started re-alizing the extractive potential of these lands. Botany started emerging as a science in the eighteenth century. Men of science began claiming for themselves the role of taxonomers and natural history experts, especially after Carl Linnaeus's system of classifying plants according to their sexual and reproductive qualities threw the shadow of immodesty over the study of botany. The stakes were suddenly higher, and naturalists, botanists, and illustrators found it much easier to get sponsored by their governments to travel on colonial expeditions.

At the same time, these expeditions were shifting their focus inland. With James Cook mapping the shores of Australia, there were no more new shores to plant the flag on. But there were entire continents, whose hinterlands were rich with natural resources, whose ecosystems needed to be mapped and surveyed and appropriated. The delicate specimens of the bougainvillea that Bougainville's expedition brought back, which can still be seen today in French herbariums, were part of this effort. Much like the journalists who were embedded with U.S. soldiers during the invasion of Iraq, natural history scholars and scientists who accompanied the explorers disguised their sympathies under the cloak of seeking and classifying and disseminating information.

In *Imperial Eyes: Travel Writing and Transculturation*, Mary Louise Pratt traces the history of modern travel writing to this particular moment. Unlike the fabulist tales of Marco Polo or the aimless adventures of Ibn Battuta, the travel writing produced in this era by natural historians is very much a surveillance project. Pratt breaks down how this travel writing comes out of a European knowledge-building project that in turn was both tool and disguise for colonial expansion. Natural history asserted the European male's authority over the planet and his rationalist, extractive understanding of people and places. It deposed a more experiential, community-oriented understanding of nature. It anointed the white male authority figure as the narrator of travel writing. Through its supposedly neutral pursuit of scientific knowledge, natural history managed to reinforce the authority of European surveillance and appropriation of resources.

The insidiousness by which natural history explorations continued the colonial project while setting themselves apart from it reminds me of how in our own times, tourists will often set themselves apart from other tourists by calling themselves travelers. While tourists are derided for their all-too-obvious desires, their kitschy souvenirs and their group tours, travelers are somehow deeper, seekers of more profound experiences. They may take the shape of voluntourists, who are convinced they are making the Third World a better place, or spiritual seekers looking to discover who they are amid the squalor. Increasingly, plain old tourism is being whitewashed and greenwashed into "travel" in the same way that mercantile exploring was reframed as natural history explorations. But these reinventions are still operating within the same voyeuristic paradigms that their predecessors set in place.

We often think of the Grand Tour as the predecessor of modern tourism. Traveling abroad taught young aristocrats how to comport themselves among other aristocrats, how to be rich and noble. For quite a few of those travelers, it was an opportunity to let their eighteenth-century hair down, far away from the stringencies and obligations of home, and perhaps pick up the latest trending venereal disease. Together, these high and low experiences broadened the cultural capital and worldliness of the Grand Tourist. The aspirations of the modern tourist—education and recreation—would seem to be pretty similar, except updated for our more democratic era.

But just as Edward Gibbon, fresh from his own Grand Tour, was sitting down to write *The History of the Decline and Fall of the Roman Empire*, Bougainville and Cook were setting out on their circumnavigations with natural historians on board. Two very different kinds of travels: both left their DNA in the tourism that we practice today in the twenty-first century and in how we talk about that tourism. While travel writing about the First World, from New York to Rome, has the same aspirational quality as the Grand Tour, travel writing about the Third World often follows the same paradigms as the natural history explorations of the eighteenth and nineteenth centuries. Both kinds of travel objectify the places being traveled to, but in predictably different patterns. One is about acquiring cultural education, whether via monuments or slow food; the other is about adventure and pseudiscovery. These are extreme binaries, and of course there are plenty of exceptions that prove the rule.

New Orleans is usually written about as an exotic Third World city while Buenos Aires gets patted on the back for being the most European city in Latin America. Istanbul straddles the middle of these binaries, much the same way that it sits geographically.

Taking travel writing to task for the many ways in which it supported the Orientalist project, Edward Said wrote in *Orientalism* how the genre used its seeming objectivity to create distinctions between the Orient and the Occident, which, in turn, reinforced the logic of imperialist expansion. This is not just the politics of travel writing; it is also its mechanics. Analyzing how white explorers of the eighteenth century created the paradigms of modern travel writing about the Third World, Pratt breaks down what she calls the "monarch-of-all-I-survey" scene. Consider, for instance, the scenes written by British explorers who went looking for the origins of the Nile in the 1860s. The point of such a scene, Pratt writes, was to produce for the home audience the peak moments at which geographical "discoveries" were "won" for England. Here's Richard Burton pseudiscovering Lake Tanganyika as published in his *The Lake Regions of Central Africa*:

> Nothing, in sooth, could be more picturesque than this first view of the Tanganyika Lake, as it lay in the lap of the mountains, basking in the gorgeous tropical sunshine. Below and beyond a short foreground of rugged and precipitous hill-fold, down which the

> foot-path zigzags painfully, a narrow strip of
> emerald green, never sere and marvelously
> fertile, shelves toward a ribbon of glistening
> yellow sand, here bordered by sedgy rushes,
> there cleanly and clearly cut by the breaking
> wavelets.

And on he goes, in painful, precipitous, glistening detail. The pseudiscovery of sites such as this involved making one's way to the region and asking the local inhabitants if they knew of any big lakes, etc., in the area, then hiring them to take you there, whereupon with their guidance and support, you proceeded to pseudiscover what they already knew. In other words, discovery equaled converting local knowledge into European discourse.

Seventeenth- and eighteenth-century European readers had an inexhaustible appetite for travel writing; perhaps they subconsciously understood the political uses of pseudiscovery. To claim by seeing was to claim by owning. What this meant was that the writer often needed to make an event out of a nonevent. The rhetoric of Burton's writing, inching slowly over the non-scene, glazing it with overwrought emotion, is ideologically astute, making a completely passive encounter into a significant national event (British explorer discovers the source of the Nile!). In order to do this effectively, the landscape must be aestheticized *and* the explorer positioned as the objective master of this landscape, the monarch of all he surveys.

It may seem from our vantage in the twenty-first century

that the travel writer has no other choice than to be a monarch of all they survey. But once we recognize this as a culturally and temporally subjective framing that emerged in the eighteenth century, as a handmaiden to colonial plunder, it becomes possible to see that there are other kinds of travel writing. What if, instead of pretending to be an objective describer of foreign landscapes and peoples, the writer accepted the limitations of their subjectivity? What if the travel writer, instead of aiming for mastery and confidence, acknowledged that travel is a terribly disorienting experience?

This was in fact the narrative stance of many medieval rihlas. Arab travelers of the Middle Ages frequently used the title *Book of Wonders* for their travelogues, Amitav Ghosh writes in his preface to *Other Routes: 1500 Years of African and Asian Travel Writing.* This book is a marvelous compendium of place-based stories from the two continents that have been the sites of so many pseudiscoveries. Ghosh writes of how ancient and medieval non-Western travel writers demonstrate a kind of meticulousness in documenting what they see and hear. He credits this to the recognition that as a foreigner in a foreign land, the writer is working beyond the borders of their common sense. Wonder is possible when the witness is willing to acknowledge the limits of their knowingness. Ghosh points out that it is this willingness to be wonderstruck that sets these accounts apart from travel writing of the kind that is guided by notions of "discovery" and "exploration." Medieval Arab travel writers "do not assume a universal ordering of reality; nor do they arrange their narratives to correspond to teleologies of racial or civilizational progress," he writes. Where the pseudiscovery tradition of travel writing appropriates travel as a tool for claiming the world imaginatively and politically, in the wonder tradition, travel is a way to test out the limitations of one's homemade knowledge and selfhood.

Unfortunately, for the most part, contemporary travel writing did not inherit the legacy of wonder. Mary Louise Pratt draws a direct line connecting the cultural script of modern travel writing with the triumphalist narratives of eighteenth-century European natural science writing. The contemporary travel writer is still painting the pseudiscovery scene except "from the balconies of hotels in third world cities," she says, citing Alberto Moravia standing on a hotel balcony in Accra describing the city as "a huge pan of thick, dark cabbage soup" in which pieces of white pasta are boiling away. Or Paul Theroux, on a hotel balcony in Guatemala City, who sees the city lying on its back, its ugliness ugliest on those streets where its blue volcanoes bulge. The difference from Burton is that both writers are aestheticizing the ugliness of the Third World city while positioning themselves as the authoritative neutral vision.

The writer Michelle Dizon and the artist Việt Lê collaborated on a marvelous photobook, *White Gaze*, which takes on the ways in which *National Geographic* magazine uses this objectifying perspective. Parodying the forms and formulas of the magazine—the yellow picture frame cover, the glossy photos, the dehumanizing captions—they lay out how it has consistently used photojournalism to reinforce a colonial vision of dark-skinned people as objects to be identified and exoticized for the benefit of a white audience. *National Geographic* has made performative attempts to reform its white gaze. In 2015, they published a photo essay on Haiti, lavishly praising themselves for using young Haitian photographers. The 2018 Race issue apologized for decades of racist coverage. Yet, like so many travel publications, it simply does not know how to let go of this cultural script. More than 75 percent of *National Geographic*'s cover stories since the apology have been assigned to white male photographers, according to an analysis conducted by *Vox* magazine. A little acknowledgement here, a little representation there only serves to fortify the white gaze. In fact, what is being pseudiscovered now is the performance of antiracism.

In a brilliant example of how pseudiscovery rewrites history, Ghosh writes of the ancient temple complex of Angkor Wat in Cambodia, which was said to have been abandoned until it was pseudiscovered by a Frenchman in the nineteenth century. But during his own visit to the monument, Ghosh spoke to a Buddhist monk and later a Cambodian archaeologist who informed him that monks had been living and worshipping in Angkor Wat for centuries before it was thus pseudiscovered. In fact after the French pseudiscovery, the monks had to resist being evicted from the complex. "It was only to Europeans then that Angkor was a discovery," Ghosh writes, but as the colonial masters of the country they were able to not only rewrite the story of the temple complex but also project themselves as the heroes of a triumphalist narrative. Sadly the myth of an abandoned temple claimed by the forest until it was discovered is much more romantic and much more salable, Ghosh writes. So the tourist industry in Cambodia has collaborated in keeping this version alive, much like the Turkish government repackaging whirling dervishes as a performance for tourists.

While visiting Angkor in 2009, the way the forest grew around and into the temples reminded me so much of the sacred groves of India. In Kerala, these are often called kaavus, and they usually contain shrines to mother goddesses. The forest runs wild around the shrines; there is no careful landscaping to ease the worshipper's path. The deep brooding silence of a kaavu, punctuated by hisses and growls, is a thing of fierce beauty and awe. Sacred groves exist all over India and in many Asian countries such as Japan and Bhutan. While the Angkor temples are part of an elegantly planned urban complex as opposed to a sacred grove, it would not have occurred to a traveler from these countries to consider a temple complex to be abandoned simply because it is surrounded by a forest. Whereas for a nineteenth-century Frenchman, steeped in the culture of urban modernity that was reshaping the West, the forest laying claim to the elegant streets of Angkor could only mean abandonment and decay. This is not just an innocent misunderstanding. Layered on top of the hasty conclusion was the paradigm of pseudiscovery, which assumes that the best thing that can happen to this strange place is pseudiscovery by a European.

•

In 1993, a manuscript was found in the Vatican Library—
The Book of Travels was a memoir of the travels of Antun
Yusuf Hanna Diyab, the Syrian man who introduced the
story of Aladdin to Europe in the early eighteenth century.
Diyab was the translator and a servant to the French naturalist and explorer Paul Lucas, who had been commissioned
to travel around the Mediterranean collecting trinkets for
the French king.

Though Lucas left multiple books about his travels, he
never mentioned Diyab, and for a long time, Diyab remained a mystery. But this newly found manuscript is an
autobiographical narrative penned by Diyab decades after
he returned to Aleppo, disillusioned by Lucas's unwilling-
ness to help him find a job in the French royal library. In the
foreword to the English translation of Diyab's *Book of Travels*, Yasmine Seale writes of how Diyab's writing "probes the
strangeness of the world." His accounts of Paris are full of
miracles jostling with daily phenomena, blurring the lines
between fiction and truth. "*The Book of Travels* smudges
such distinctions by showing how fantasy is woven into
life, how enchantment is neighbor to inquiry," Seale writes.
Reading this, I am reminded of how distinctly this paradigm of wonder—of recognizing the unknowability of the
world—distinguishes itself from the paradigm of pseudiscovery. Wonder emerges from a willingness to see the
other not as something to be explained but as something
that cannot be fully understood within the limitations of
the traveler's subjectivity.

Such self-awareness and humility would be dismissed

as naivete and lack of sophistication in the kind of travel writing that inherited the mantle of the eighteenth-century exploring narrator-savant. In a tongue-in-cheek essay upbraiding the Indian male for various bad habits, Mukul Kesavan writes:

> Travel writing, as invented by English and then American writers, is a form of amused knowingness. Reading Robert Byron or Paul Theroux is a bit like tuning into Radio Supercilious: the funny bits, such as they are, are generated by the discomfort of travelling to out-of-the-way places or via encounters with amusing aboriginals. This form of knowingness isn't easily replicated: you have to be first world and better off than the natives.

It is the abandonment of this knowingness, an embrace of the subaltern perspective, that makes for insightful travel writing that moves beyond the narrative superciliousness. Kesavan points to Amitav Ghosh's *In an Antique Land*, alongside Vikram Seth's *From Heaven Lake* and Allan Sealy's *From Yukon to Yucatan*, as works that redefine the travel-writing genre because "these writers treat the landscapes they move through as dense, real places, not as props and cues that help the sophisticated traveller rehearse his world-weary routines."

I find it hard to take seriously travel writing that does

not question its own assumptions. I am drawn to travel narrators who parse their place in the world thoughtfully, whose marginalities give them offbeat insights into a changing world. I do not take seriously the distinction between traveler and expat and migrant, which is yet another way in which racial and economic privilege is hammered into place. Some of my favorite travel narratives are from what Aminatta Forna refers to as the "been-to" genre: books written by African writers who went abroad and returned to tell the tale. Others are journalistic deep dives that parse the interconnections between culture and economy, food and politics, leisure and climate, luxury and inequality. More and more I find the travel stories I love best are not on the bookshelf labeled TRAVEL. They are, perhaps, in a finely detailed detective novel where the writer pays attention to how a neighborhood is laid out, its invisible social logics and rituals. Or in poetry, where contradiction and confusion have always found a safe refuge.

But as a child, and like many children who are obsessed with geography and world capitals and maps, I too fattened my imagination on the corpus of travel writing that was easily available to me. I read book after book in which the standard-issue pale male set out on a journey. This was, after all, the majority of travel books. I inserted myself into the adventures of Robert Louis Stevenson's sailors and *Swiss Family Robinson*, a gateway toward the suaveness of Patrick Leigh Fermor and the flamboyance of Bruce Chatwin. As a grown-up, I used to feel ashamed that despite the narrative injustices by which people who look like me were always

Calibans and Man Fridays, I had somehow managed to identify with the narrators of these white travel stories.

But now I realize I was simply being a bougainvillea. A bract pretending to be a flower, while secretly keeping its soft heart safe, waiting to read Jamaica Kincaid's letter to Robinson Crusoe: "Dear Mr. Crusoe, Please stay home."

In 2019, three hundred years after Daniel Defoe published *Robinson Crusoe*, Jamaica Kincaid wrote an introduction to a new edition of the book that launched a thousand ships. How bracing to read Kincaid's sharp-witted epistle to Crusoe. "There's no need for this ruse of going on a trading journey, in which more often than not the goods you are trading are people like me," she writes. Like many of us whose small-town libraries were full of dog-eared copies of *Treasure Island* and *Robinson Crusoe*, Kincaid, too, grew up reading colonial tales of swagger and danger set amid the noble and not-so-noble savages.

In fact, there's a place Robinson Crusoe didn't come to. Ernakulam, where I grew up. He came to Fort Kochi, just a few miles away, and it shows. The Portuguese, the Dutch, and the British have left their marks on Fort Kochi. Today it is a charming town full of colonial architecture and pretty bougainvillea-lined streets and trellised balconies, where vendors line the streets and beaches, selling you wooden beads, caftans, sun hats, brass lamps, seashell toys. Ernakulam is the rain-shadow zone of all this cuteness. It is all business. Cell phone repair shops and sari emporiums and discount malls and steel wholesalers and parking lots and flyovers and billboards featuring larger-than-life celebrities. Instead of bougainvillea climbing the walls, electric wiring is everywhere, draped around telephone poles and festooned over hospitals.

When I was a teenager, I loved sneaking away to Fort Kochi. Its artsy cafés and air-conditioned hotels and beaches and seafood shacks were a refuge from the grimness and busyness of Ernakulam. I loved skipping classes to take the dangerously overloaded commuter ferry to Fort Kochi. Friends who lived there seemed to have much more glamorous lives, walking casually back to their homes on streets shaded by the canopies of massive rain trees, brought from Brazil by the Portuguese. When they ran out to buy soap or milk, they passed Vasco da Gama's tomb! Chinese fishing nets! The basilica and the synagogue! Tourists wandered around with eyes dazed from the surfeit of history and beauty.

Fort Kochi is one of the great successes of Kerala's tourism makeover. While Ernakulam played catch-up with India's über-cities, Kerala's long and narrow coast was getting a makeover as part of a tourism policy that kicked into gear in the early 1980s and was in full throttle in the 1990s. Within what seemed like a handful of years, long stretches of the Arabian Sea coast in Kerala transformed from the natural habitat of Kerala's fishing communities into Western-style beaches where mostly white foreigners came to get tans and drink fruity cocktails. Kerala had taken a long hard look at Goa up the coast and thought, *If them, why not us?* Until then, the beaches were usually evening destinations for local families and vaynokkis: they were where you went to feel the breeze, as the day cooled down. Maybe get some peanuts or ice cream. Fishing boats would bob in the water as the sun set. But for the foreign tourists, many of them desperately escaping the freeze and slush of their home countries, the beach was where you spent the day. One by one, the beaches of Kerala fell to them, like tiny kingdoms getting annexed: Kovalam, Kochi, Varkala.

We enjoyed the tourists very much. They were so different from us, and their strange complexions and their behaviors made them fun to watch. Some of them were snobs and some of them were kind and some of them were clueless. In other words, they were human, like us. But there was one way in which they were not like us: they had money. Not all of us were poor, but in the 1980s and '90s, even those of us who had money did not spend it quite as freely as the tourists did. And their money slowly changed livelihoods on the beaches. Fishing families turned to tourist trades, running small guesthouses and thatched-roof restaurants. Young men put gel in their hair and became tourist guides. Some of them started finding jobs in the big hotels and resorts that then started coming up. Real estate prices started going up near beaches, and many beaches, until then public property, somehow became private.

Like many Malayalis, I felt proud of Kerala's reputation as a tourist paradise while also rolling my eyes at the tag line invented by the Tourism Development Corporation: "Kerala: God's Own Country." Malayalis joked that there should be an addendum to this: "Devil's Own People." We became "locals"—sometimes kindly locals, sometimes rapacious

locals. "Don't give me tourist prices," we said when bargain-
ing in markets or shops near hotels. I felt embarrassed then
when I saw vendors openly squeezing money out of hapless
white people. There is a conspiracy between service provid-
ers in little tourist towns. With the straightest of faces, a
vendor will charge two hundred rupees for a bag of stale
spices that has been sitting out in the sun for months, while
right behind her, the auto-rickshaw driver will sincerely offer a bargain fare of five hundred rupees for a ride around
town that is mostly the same loop of three or four 500-year-
old this and 300-year-old that. Sometimes they would catch
each other's eyes and they would exchange one-tenth of a
smile and a head shake. I learned quickly never to take an
auto-rickshaw from the yellow-brick roads of Fort Kochi.

Now, when I visit Fort Kochi, I feel proud of these
shenanigans. When I see the teenagers who hang out on
beaches asking tourists whether they want a sunset cruise
without mentioning that it is on the local commuter ferry
or the woman at the beach shack pretending that the fish in
her shop has been just freshly caught in the Chinese fishing
nets and did not come out of an icebox, I think, *Yes, take
their money.* The hypnotic rhythms of the Chinese fishing
nets moving up and down are mostly for show anyway. The
waters around Fort Kochi are depleted of fish thanks to
overfishing and pollution, caused, in part, by tourism gone
wild. One could think of the price gouging as a form of reparation, but it has also resulted in inflation and gentrifica-
tion that then makes places like Fort Kochi unaffordable for
its own people.

Which is why I now appreciate Ernakulam. Far-better food awaits you in the charmless food courts of Ernakulam's malls and its linoleum-lined restaurants and the roadside stands where commuters catch a rushed bite leaning out of cars and scooters. Ernakulam is dusty and jumbled, with zero cobbled streets. Ernakulam is the stepsister whose job is to clean and cook and fetch. Robinson Crusoe is not interested in Ernakulam. This is why Ernakulam feels like a refuge now, a place that does not have to pretend to be stuck in a historic time period.

As a child, I would often hear some families described as "old families." The bride or groom is from an "old family," someone would say at a wedding. This was said in a hushed tone of awe and respect, to convey prestige and lineage. If a family could trace its lineage back many generations, then it must be very respectable. My extremely literal brain would wonder: *Isn't every family old, since we all have ancestors?* Slowly I understood that the old families were the ones who had managed to keep records of themselves and their exploits. Historic districts such as Fort Kochi now strike me as "old families." Surely places like Ernakulam are also historic, since there must have been some kind of life taking place in Ernakulam at the same time that colonial buildings were going up in Fort Kochi. But of course, "historic," like "old family," is a testament to whether a place or a family was important enough to be documented. Which should leave us wondering, by what measures are some places and some people not important?

Yet not bearing the burden of history has certainly been

a boon for Ernakulam. Its very banality has saved it from
being a simulacrum of its past self. It has other problems,
of course. It is a marvelously ugly city, with its flyovers and
skyscrapers and huge billboards. But what a relief it is to
be in a place where the marigold garlands go on idols in
temples and not around tourists' necks. The tailors are all
booked for months; no one is going to sew you a colorful
Indian tunic while you wait. When the bus stops at the traffic jam just before Jos Junction and the conductor calls out
"half Jos, half Jos" in case someone wants to get off there, it
doesn't matter if no one gets the joke; he did it for himself,
not for a Tripadvisor review.

Elsewhere I am the tourist. And when I am elsewhere, I,
too, appreciate the convenient way in which the ecosystem
of a tourist district will wrap itself conveniently around my
needs. I buy overpriced souvenirs and I follow the bright
arrows on tourist maps and I read Tripadvisor reviews. But
I also have a newfound respect for the Ernakulams of the
world. The unhistoric districts. Sometimes a town, sometimes a suburb, sometimes something in between. You catch
sight of them from the window of a train perhaps, while
moving from one famous town to the other, or maybe you
were out on a walk and got a bit lost and went farther afield
than the map told you to. Nothing there to see, someone
will tell you back at the hotel. Just . . . schools and houses
and hospitals and the other boring stuff of life.

So, dear Mr. Crusoe, don't come to Ernakulam. There
is nothing to see here. Don't bother with the waterfront
at Marine Drive, where young couples with nowhere else

to go carve out slivers of privacy under umbrellas. Avoid the fish-and-vegetable market that sits astride the dirty canal that feeds into the backwater. Do not walk down Broadway, which is actually so narrow a couple of auto-rickshaws could cause a traffic jam. Ignore completely Mather Street, which is about two feet wide, with its cluster of craft and sewing shops. A few years ago, I went with my mother one day to her favorite shop for restocking on embroidery doodads, and as I was sitting on a rickety plastic stool, I heard the vaanku and looked on Google Maps to see which mosque it was coming from, and I saw on my screen, tucked amid the tiny alleys in this part of the town, among hosiery shops and hardware stores, surrounded by the stench of the nearby fish market, three places of worship: Kadavumbagam Synagogue, Central Juma Masjid, and Saint Antony's Church, all within half a mile of one another. A tiny Jerusalem, for quick prayers stolen from daily working lives. "One minute, auntie; keep an eye on this for me," our vendor said as he threw a skullcap on his head and joined the row of young men who had risen from the sewing shops to make their way to the mosque for prayers. We waited, my mother and I, keeping an eye on the rainbow and steel arrays of threads and bobbins and embroidery kits and scissors, and I thought of how sewing shops and fish markets rarely make it into history. What a loss that is, and also—how fortunate for them.

Chapter

SEVEN

✈

SEVERAL YEARS AGO, WHEN I HAD JUST MOVED TO NEW York, my mother called me up and told me that she had found a couple of broke European tourists who were having trouble figuring out how to change their traveler's checks. They were standing at a bank counter trying to sort out all the paperwork. My mother helped them fill out the forms in triplicate and photocopy their passports. When she understood how little money they had, she invited them home for lunch. After feeding them, she asked, per ancient Indian custom, if they would like to take an afternoon nap. When they woke up from their naps, she served them coffee and snacks. Then she sent them on their way with advice and banana chips. "Your father was very annoyed about it all," she told me, "but I thought, my own children are in other countries. I hope someone helps them when they need help." My mother is the kind stranger that other mothers hope their children will find when they travel abroad. Whenever I encounter any good fortune on my own travels, I think of my mother and how she eased the road for those two hapless travelers.

If my father hated travel, my mother could not get enough of it. She enjoys new places, new people, new things to do.

It is entirely possible that my parents were only slightly different from each other in their travel preferences when they began their marriage as impressionable twentysomethings. But marriages have a way of exacerbating polarities, with the two selves constructing themselves against each other. And so whether it was my mother resisting my father's crustiness or whether it was my father scaling back against my mother's enthusiasm, their polarities shaped my own childhood.

It was my mother who took our family traveling. Most of her meager salary went toward rent and school fees. But one of the benefits of my mother's job in a government bank was that her employer paid for employees to visit their hometowns. Local employees, like my mother, used this benefit for touristic travel. So every few years, our family, armed with canisters of drinking water and pickles and podis to add zest to railway meals, boarded a train at Ernakulam Railway Station. We visited Delhi, Agra, Bangalore, Madras, Bombay, sleeping overnight in trains, making friends out of fellow passengers, eating fabulous unrepeatable meals I can only dream of now as multiple families shared their tiffin boxes and passed around pickle jars.

We made friends on the train easily, thanks to my mother. As soon as she got settled in her seat, my mother would turn to the stranger next to her and smile warmly. "So. Where to?" she would begin, while the introverts in our family averted their eyes painfully. Luckily, her curiosity is matched by her charm. Everyone in the world is waiting to tell my mother their life story. I would pretend to read, but secretly I was always listening. The new parents on a pilgrimage to thank a Sufi saint and the Virgin Mother, for blessing them after five miscarriages. A policewoman who married a man she arrested. A nun who survived a war zone.

I was listening as these strangers told their stories, but really, I was listening to the stranger that my mother became on the train. Who was this funny, charming, relaxed woman? At home, my mother was strict and practical, helpfully informing us that time wasted could not ever be regained. I could always hear her making mental to-do lists. But on the train, her whole body became soft. All the lower-middle-class anxieties about paying English medium school fees and looking respectable at weddings slithered away, leaving a mother who laughed easily, a mother who listened without judgment, a mother who wasted time.

But it's not a waste of time, my mother will retort after reading this. Conversations with strangers are how my mother figures out the correct taxi fare to pay when she gets to her destination, where to buy T-shirts at wholesale prices, which companies are hiring engineering graduates in which towns—thus, over the course of a hundred train journeys, she has become the auntie to call when you need information.

"Look, amooomma is making a new best friend," my daughter whispers to me when my mother turns to the unsuspecting stranger next to her with a nuclear disarmament–level smile. It doesn't always work. If you are the young man on the shuttle train to Kottayam trying to read *Love in the Time of Cholera*, circa July 2018, please accept my apologies.

I, too, always carry a book, not so much to read but as a totem that wards off unwanted conversationalists. Unlike my mother, many train conversationalists are talkers, not listeners. My body can sense when I am sitting next to a mansplainer before he opens his mouth.

My fear of being captured by a transportation conversationalist goes hand in hand with my horror of turning into one. What could be more uncool? Giving people their space, maintaining our own bubbles of quiet—this is how we demonstrate our worldliness as travelers. And the more travel becomes intertwined with technology, the more individualistic travel fantasies become, the more gauche it is to talk to your fellow travelers. Still, what to do with the humanity that sometimes bubbles up, despite all one's attempts to be suave and mysterious? Sometimes when I settle into a seat and feel the texture of time itself changing, I turn to the person sitting next to me. Here we are. Two strangers brought together. Two histories intersecting. We may be stuck here for eternity. I see you, your youness. Tell me everything. Instead of all that, I say, "So. Where to?"

A long-distance train snaking across a vast continent: this will forever be my utopian ideal of a journey, thanks to my mother. Even my anti-travel father gets a little misty-eyed when we talk about those train journeys that he was forced to go on. I learned the geography of India through the foods that vendors thrust through our windows in the frantic minutes that the train stopped at railway stations along the way: banana fritters at Palakkad, curd rice in Coimbatore, fresh juice at the massive Vijayawada station where we also refilled our water, baskets of oranges in Nagpur that someone had to be deputed to stay up for since the trains from Kerala arrived at Nagpur at midnight, cool sweet white pedas at Mathura and the shock with which I found out they were made of ash gourd, the high-pitched wail of the cucumber vendor as he walked through the train with his shaker of mixed spice powders to dress the thick cool strips of cucumbers we longed for when the train fans stopped working, and samosas with a side of fiery green chilies that announced firmly that the train had now entered the strange and unpredictable territories known to us South Indians as North India.

In the essay collection *Black Coffee in a Coconut Shell: Caste as Lived Experience*, the writer A. Chinnadurai writes: "Normally, during [train] journeys I prefer not to talk to strangers because it would finally lead to the question on caste or they would make efforts to somehow find out my caste." He then relates an incident on a train journey in which an old man in spotless white clothes wearing kumkum on his forehead tries to find out what caste Chinnadurai belongs to. At first the questions are subtle—what do you do for work, who is your clan deity—but after Chinnadurai expertly fends off these questions, the old man finally blurts out: "Are you . . . a Harijan?" When Chinnadurai eventually replies that he belongs to the Adi Dravidar community, the old man refuses to believe it, because Chinnadurai is educated and well spoken. "I know how people look," he says to justify himself.

I know how we looked as a family. Nothing about us signaled Muslim except our names—my father and brother with their clean-shaven faces, my mother and sister and I with our uncovered heads. Looking back, I believe this had so much to do with our happy experiences on the train. The books we read, the music we listened to, the mostly vegetarian foods we ate all said "good Muslim." We did not set out to appear so harmless, but then again, maybe we did without realizing what we were doing. Once, when returning from a college trip with friends, our train stopped at Coimbatore station, the day after bomb blasts had claimed six lives there. The platform was crawling with cops. Sitting in a window seat, I wound a scarf around my head to shield myself from the sun. A friend teased me, "Stop it, you look like a terrorist." I laughed obligingly.

In July 2023, a railway officer aboard a train hailed Prime Minister Narendra Modi, then killed four men, three of whom were Muslims. All three Muslims were men who looked Muslim. I pored over their pictures, the beards and the white kurtas, and thought of the many beloved cousins and uncles who looked like them.

Perhaps the reason I romanticize those childhood train journeys is because they belong to a world I cannot return to. Over the course of my own life, India has become a dangerous place to be Muslim. I used to keep track of the normalization of Islamophobia on social media by friends and friends of friends and teachers, till the trickle became a deluge and tracking became impossible and pointless. Perhaps this is why I luxuriate in memories of those long train rides. How boldly the train threw eight random Indians together into a compartment, filling compartment after compartment thus for half a kilometer, and made us all share bathrooms and offer one another our food. And it gave us its own inefficiency as a gift, something to bond over.

And perhaps this world I remember is a child's memory of childhood, sheltered by parents who protected us from hostile interactions. After all, our trains have been the sites of enormous communal trauma, from the Partition-era trains that arrived in Pakistan and India with only corpses, to the train in Godhra that Muslims were accused of burning down before Gujarat became a bloodbath. So maybe all I am saying is this: there were a few days in my childhood when the trains showed me what to dream about as an adult.

It was on the train that I first began obsessing over exactly when the present and the past collide. Did the place that you just saw out of the window belong to the past? What if you just walked back to a train car that was reaching that place just then? Did that count as time travel? How strange that the present in which you were thinking about the past had suddenly become past. Sometimes at a bend in the rails, I would see the awe-inspiring sight of the length of the train on both sides, curving gently. What I had thought of as a straight line was much more twisted. What did this mean for time?

Often, the train would pause for hours in the middle of a lush valley or on a dry plain surrounded by brush for hundreds of kilometers. Sometimes we would make an unscheduled stop at some tiny railway station, waiting for a train from the opposite direction to pass us. Sometimes someone would pull the chain, grinding the train to a halt; once it was a woman who panicked that someone had cut her gold chain off her neck while she was sleeping; it turned out she had forgotten that she took it off and secreted it in a suitcase before her nap. Sometimes, especially during the monsoons, the train would move very cautiously through waterlogged valleys lest a sudden movement set off a landslide. My point is, time became elastic during those train journeys. None of us expected to reach wherever we were going on time.

·

Time was the first of many things I found suspicious about *Around the World in Eighty Days*. The Jules Verne novel, published in 1872, starts off with Phileas Fogg wagering twenty thousand pounds with his friends at the Reform Club in London that he would be able to circumnavigate the world in less than three months. Fogg, an independently wealthy British gentleman, is confident that he will be able to traverse the entire world and return to the club in exactly eighty days. Off he goes with his French valet, Jean Passepartout, on an adventure that takes him from England to France to Italy to Egypt to India to Hong Kong to Japan to the United States and back to London. The novel is the third in a series of adventure travel fiction by Jules Verne, all of them inspired by the immense technological advances that were occurring in the nineteenth century.

As a child reading this book, I was mesmerized by the names of places that Fogg travels to. But I counted them and it just didn't make sense that this itinerary of eight or nine different places, barely touching Africa, completely ignoring South America and Australia, could be considered travel around the world. As I grew up, I kept returning to the book with more questions. For instance, how did Phileas Fogg make his money? Right at the beginning, Verne makes a point of how no one knows where Fogg's wealth came from. He has no need for anything as undignified as work; he has never been seen at the exchange or at the bank or in the city or in any of the courts; he was not a manufacturer or a trader or a merchant or a gentleman farmer. Unlike Jane Austen, who tells us exactly how many pounds a year her characters live on and where it comes from, Verne shrugs and informs us that Fogg's wealth just is.

But he is English and this is not a coincidence: the English were the most assertive travelers at the beginning of the modern era. "Ours is a nation of travelers," the British poet Samuel Rogers wrote in 1830. Or as Lawrence Osborne puts it in his 2006 book *The Naked Tourist*, the British were the ugly Americans of the eighteenth century.

Where did this British fervor to see the world come from? Prior to the Industrial Revolution, travel was a luxury. The Grand Tour is a famous example. But starting in the middle of the eighteenth century, the rise of manufacturing wealth also created a new class of consumers in Britain.

It wasn't just that the Industrial Revolution made tourism possible; it also made it necessary. Everyday life during the Industrial Revolution was filled with oppressive indignities and unheard-of comforts. Eric Zuelow writes in *A History of Modern Tourism* of how pollution and overcrowding became normal as whole new cities mushroomed almost overnight and people flooded into these growing urban centers. Trash was everywhere. Coal smoke poured out of the factories as well as the overcrowded housing. There was no running water until the second half of the nineteenth century. As everyday life became more miserable while technology and buying power advanced, a vacation in the mountains or at the beach slowly became possible and necessary for more and more people.

"Before the mid-eighteenth century, people simply did not go into the mountains if they could help it," Zuelow writes. According to travel historians, it was the German Romantics, closely followed by the English, who first took to the mountains. Perhaps the picture that represents this moment best is Caspar David Friedrich's *Wanderer Above the Sea of Fog* (1818), in which we see, from the back, a man in a green coat standing atop a craggy rock, looking into a misty valley. He is alone. He is thinking. He is on a mountain. The man personifies this very eighteenth-century Western European yearning to get away and climb the mountains. A word was invented to express this desire by compounding the German words *wandern* (*hike*) and *lust* (*desire*): *wanderlust*.

"Two weeks before the end of the [eighteenth] century, a brother and sister went walking across the snow," Rebecca Solnit writes in *Wanderlust: A History of Walking*. The brother is William and the sister is Dorothy. The Wordsworth siblings were walking across the Pennine mountains of northern England over the course of four days to their new home in Grasmere, Lake District. Solnit relates what an extraordinary act this was—walking, not out of necessity, but as an aesthetic experience. Soon the British middle class, flush with wealth from industrialization and eager for a respite from the dizzying rate of urbanization, followed

Wordsworth and other Romantics into the mountains. Alpine mountaineering would go on to become one of the first sites of modern tourist activity. Climbing clubs started erupting around Europe, with the first one established in London in 1857. As tourism took off, wanderlust evolved and came to mean the desire to travel, not just in the mountains and not simply by walking. There is a bread-crumb trail leading from the eighteenth century's search for the sublime in the mountains to the popularity of #wanderlust on Instagram today.

The beach was the other space that transformed into a recreational site over the course of the eighteenth century. According to beach historians—yes, this is a real job—the medievals did not have much use for oceans. The seas were nasty and dangerous, associated with seasickness, monsters, and mythical disasters. The beach was where invasions began and soldiers departed for war. But in eighteenth- and nineteenth-century Britain, beaches acquired an aspirational gloss. After George III was prescribed sea dipping as a cure for his porphyria in 1789, sea bathing became popular among the upper classes, and a sea-bathing machine was invented to enable the upper classes, especially women, to enter the waters without being gawked at. The machines were like mobile chariots that could be wheeled into the ocean, allowing the person inside an opportunity to dip into the water while preserving their modesty.

I first came across sea-bathing machines in Jane Austen's unfinished novel, *Sanditon*, a sharply vivid portrait of a Victorian seaside town in the frenzy of becoming a beach destination. Austen started writing this novel in the early nineteenth century. By the second half of the nineteenth century, beach culture was in full swing. Here's some first-hand testimony from *Alice's Adventures in Wonderland*, published in 1865: "Alice had been to the seaside once in her life and had come to the general conclusion that, wherever you go to on the English coast, you find a number of bathing machines in the sea, some children digging in the sand with wooden spades, then a row of lodging houses, and behind them a railway station."

I have often thought that going to the beach is just not worth everything I have to lug there. Blanket, sunscreen, snacks, books, swimsuit, towel, drinking water, sun hats, friends . . . But the sea-bathing machine makes this list look like nothing. It involved an umbrella, a box, sometimes a horse to pull the machine or a complex rope-and-pulley system. And servants who were required to run this contraption and hand around sandwiches afterward.

Consider the sandwich, supposedly invented in 1762, just in time for those mountain hikes and beach picnics. Its creation is credited to John Montagu, the 4th Earl of Sandwich, who asked for a meal that could be eaten one-handed during a gambling binge. Based on my reading of P. G. Wodehouse's Jeeves books, I am going to assume that the earl had nothing to do with the actual making; it was his cook or some other minion who put the meat between the two pieces of bread. But even before we arrive at that fateful gambling binge, chances are that the earl and his cook were inspired by his travels in the Mediterranean, where mezze platters featured bread wrapped around dips and cheeses and meats. In *Sandwich: A Global History*, Bee Wilson writes of how sandwiches had existed for thousands of years before the Earl of Sandwich ate them, whether in French peasant food or Jewish Passover meals. In other words, an English aristocrat is credited with inventing the sandwich when, in reality, what he did was make it popular in a place where he had the cultural capital to have it named after him.

Often while reading the history of tourism, I wonder how much of it is a colonial knowledge sandwich. Were the beaches in the Pacific taboo to the coastal people who lived there, in the same way that European beaches were taboo in the Middle Ages? We know now that it was the Polynesians who taught the world the art of surfing—Joseph Banks, the naturalist aboard the Cook expedition, describes how Tahitian swimmers would ride the waves using the stem of an old canoe. Did no one really go walking in the mountains till Wordsworth did? After all, mountains around the world are home to Indigenous communities whose stories have been excluded and dismissed from mainstream histories for generations, from the Lakota on the Black Hills of South Dakota to the Samburu and Maasai people who live on Mount Nyiru in Kenya. In *Wild*, Jay Griffiths writes about how Indigenous communities speak of the mountains they live on with reverence and affection, whereas mountaineering literature is full of the vocabulary of war, military might, imperialism, nationalism, and masculinity. Men were always "conquering" mountains or "laying siege to them," she points out, quoting writer after writer, from Ronald William Clark, who wrote of beating the alpine summit into submission, to H. B. George, who wrote that the desire "to explore the Earth and subdue it" had "made England the great colonizer of the world." Compared to that, Griffiths says, many Indigenous traditions view the mountains as female, a mothering deity.

My friend Janelle Trees, a traveling doctor who worked for years in the central Australian desert, often spoke wearily about the climbers who come to Uluru, the sacred rock of the Pitjantjatjara community who live around Uluru. Uluru is part of the traditional rituals of the Pitjantjatjara, who consider themselves the custodians of the rock. Janelle calls Uluru "one of the most frequently and profoundly misunderstood places on a hundred thousand bucket lists." Uluru was pseudiscovered in 1873 by William Gosse, who named it after an Australian politician, Henry Ayers. The colonial Australian government promoted Ayers Rock as a tourist destination in the same way that the United States has used tourism to take away Indigenous lands and turn them into national parks. Uluru soon became one of those unfortunate places that millions of travelers around the world were told is a must-see-before-you-die. In direct opposition to the wishes of the Pitjantjatjara, these tourists insisted on climbing Uluru. As a doctor in the tiny desert clinic that was meant primarily for serving the local Aboriginal community, Janelle and her staff of three nurses often found themselves catering instead to climbers who had to be rescued after they lost their way among the clefts within Uluru or fell into a rock hole or developed extreme heat stroke. In 2019, after decades of advocacy by Australian

Aboriginal activists, the Australian government finally banned the climbing of Uluru.

Even the tallest peak in the world is not immune from tragedies brought on by the self-aggrandizement of tourism. In May 2019, Mount Everest witnessed one of its deadliest seasons, with eleven climbers freezing to death as they crowded on the tiny summit, 8,850 meters above sea level. *The New York Times* interviewed a man who survived that climb: he had to step around the corpse of a woman who had not.

The photo the *Times* published alongside this article—a long line of climbers in brightly colored snow gear against an expanse of white mountain—popped into my head when I read the very first page of *Fallen Giants*, Stewart Weaver and Maurice Isserman's 2008 book on the history of mountaineering in the Himalayas. "Mountain climbing is a sport without spectators and, particularly in the Himalaya, the climbers are almost always the only ones on the scene to witness and record their triumphs and tragedies," the authors wrote. This is no longer true. Two years after that sentence was published, Apple introduced the iPhone 4, with its front-facing camera. Since then, the selfie has become ritualized into tourism, and mountaineering, too, has become a sport in self-spectatorship. During climbing season, it is now de rigueur to wait in a long line to take a selfie at the very top.

While mountaineering was turning into a popular Western pastime in nineteenth-century Europe, the British were establishing "hill stations" all over India. In Shimla, Darjeeling, Mussorie, Ooty, the formula was the same: roads were cleared, bungalows were built, clock towers and fountains and statues popped up, and boarding schools for European children mushroomed. The hill stations were a reprieve from the hard work of colonizing, so they were built to simulate a home away from home. This is the root of the morphological resemblance between Indian hill stations and nineteenth-century English villages. While writers such as Rudyard Kipling tended to paint the hill stations as quixotic places, far removed from the brutality of colonialism, in reality, as Dane Kennedy writes in *The Magic Mountains*, "these places were profoundly engaged in the complex refractory processes of colonialism."

I had to pause and sit with my confusion when I first read this. I love the hill stations of India, their quaint little rituals and the eye-cooling vistas offered by the lines of their gardens. And yet so many of these rituals and vistas—the club libraries that will not let any adult male enter unless he is wearing shoes, the assembly lines in which tea plantations are laid out, the magnificent veranda views from the plantation houses that ensure optimum surveillance of workers—are grounded in the colonial politics of exclusion and exploitation. The more we dig into the history of modern tourism, the more the pickax hits its underground cable connection with colonialism.

When I read that the first Alpine Club was established in London in 1857, the date rang a bell. The year marked the Indian Rebellion of 1857, also referred to as the Sepoy Mutiny in British history. The coincidence is a reminder that the furious pace at which tourism was developing in Europe was taking place alongside an equally furious pace of colonization in Asia and Africa. The economic expansion that enabled European tourism was fueled by colonization. The Industrial Revolution could not have taken place without raw materials from the colonies or indentured labor that could be transported easily between colonies.

Consider for instance Manila hemp. You may have come across this versatile material in your tea bag. A product extracted from the abaca plant (a relative of the banana plant), it is indigenous to the Philippines. The strong waterproof tensile fiber extracted from the abaca plant was traditionally used for making clothing in the Philippine Islands. After the Spanish colonization was followed by the U.S. takeover, Manila hemp became a crucial export item. It was used to make lightweight waterproof rope that was used for rigging ships and dragging machine pulleys. For the merchant navies and battleships of the nineteenth-century colonial empires, Manila hemp was key to safety and efficiency, as essential as the lascars, the underpaid crewmen hired in the colonies. The London Alpine Club established its credentials by creating a strong, lightweight waterproof mountain rope using three strands of Manila hemp.

Manila hemp is one of hundreds of tropical products that began getting cultivated as large-scale monocrops by European colonizers in Asia, Africa, and South America. Typically, this involved cutting down vast swaths of tropical forests and moving huge numbers of slaves or indentured laborers from populated colonies to new plantation economies. From cotton in the American South to sugar in Barbados to tea in India to rubber in Malaysia, the profits from the plantation agricultural complex undergirded European economies during the Industrial Revolution. One could call this trade, but given the inequality built into the relationship between the two parties, historians from colonized countries have identified it more accurately as plunder. Plantation agriculture also provided a template for a sophisticated economic operation in which output is maximized through low wages, division of labor, and repetitive tasks. It anticipated the assembly-line factory system. Thus, colonialism not only helped fund capitalism but also provided a production model.

It will never cease to amaze me how little this is talked about outside academia when we talk about the history of European Everything. There I am watching *The Great British Bake Off*, perhaps the feel-goodest program in the history of television. One of the hosts is interviewing a bread historian. Medieval British bread was chewy, the historian tells her, but with the arrival of sugar, bread could be fermented more easily.

The arrival of sugar. How innocuous that sounds, as if sugar decided one day to go on a trip to Britain. However, as Sidney Mintz put it in *Sweetness and Power*: "England fought the most, conquered the most colonies, imported the most slaves . . . and went furthest and fastest in creating a plantation system. The most important product of that system was sugar." From the middle of the seventeenth century, when Britain colonized Barbados and Jamaica, well into the beginning of the twentieth century, the Caribbean was the most important source of sugar for England, which used its

maritime power to transport African slaves and Indian indentured laborers to the Caribbean sugar plantations and
then import the molasses they produced into England. The
profits of this triangular trade led to the emergence of an
English bourgeoisie and enabled a range of recreational joys
from baking to tourism. It should not be possible to talk
of how Europe invented modernity without talking about
these tiny objects—sugar, silk, Manila hemp, coffee, to-
bacco, cotton, tea, indigo, spices—that enriched Europe and
triggered the fossil-fuel-based consumption economy that is
destroying the planet today.

It should also not be possible to talk of how the British inaugurated modern tourism without talking about the other
global travel of that time. Between 1700 and 1808, British
and American merchants sent ships to gather enslaved people from six regions of Africa: Senegambia, Sierra Leone/
Windward Coast, Gold Coast, the Bight of Benin, the Bight
of Biafra, and West Central Africa. These ships carried the
captives primarily to the British sugar islands (where more
than 70 percent of them were sold, almost half of these in
Jamaica), but a sizable number were also sent to French and
Spanish buyers, and about one in ten was shipped to various
North American destinations.

In *The Slave Ship: A Human History*, Marcus Rediker
writes of the many creative and life-affirming ways in which
the multiethnic Black people who were enslaved and transported in slave ships found community. They created new
hybrid languages and cultures and fashioned new forms
of kinship to replace what had been lost when they were

abducted. Over the course of four centuries, 12.4 million Black people were trafficked, of whom 10.8 million survived the Atlantic Passage, dispersing into the populations of the Americas, the Caribbean, and Europe.

After enslaved people were emancipated in the 1830s, the British solved the labor problem by using "coolies" from South Asia as well as China and the Pacific Islands. In Malayalam, my mother tongue, *coolie* means "daily wages." In English, it came to mean "the indentured laborer, transported across British colonies to work in plantations for little to no wages." In *Coolie Woman*, Gaiutra Bahadur writes of how, over the course of eight decades, the British ferried more than a million "coolies" to more than a dozen colonies. Many of these workers did not fully understand where they were going or what they were getting paid. They worked in sugarcane plantations all over the Caribbean, helped build railways in Africa, and served in colonial households. The reason the British tourist has an outsize place in the history of travel as the first tourists of the modern age is because of this other travel: ships full of human beings, abducted and indentured.

Several years ago, I took the Main Line train from Kandy to Colombo in Sri Lanka. This is one of the most scenic train rides in the world. It was a morning train, and many of my fellow passengers, on their way to the plains to begin the workweek, had sleep in their eyes as they swayed to the train's movements. As the train twisted its way down rain-washed green hills, it passed tea gardens and waterfalls and temples. Suddenly rounding a cliff, it almost seemed to defy gravity and my heart beat a little faster. But nobody else on the train was worried. Elsewhere on that line, at the Demodara Loop, the train track winds around itself in a miracle of civil engineering. The train leaves the station and then enters a tunnel that is situated under that station in order to descend the hill as efficiently as possible. Legend has it that the Sri Lankan engineer responsible for envisioning this got the idea after watching a Tamil indentured laborer tie his turban securely, looping one end under the fabric.

The train is the ultimate metaphor for the long aftermath of colonialism, the tracks it leaves across the landscape of the colonized country, from mountain to port, the way it loops and twists to accommodate itself while creating a seemingly straight narrative of colonial public good. As my train glissaded its way from the hill station to the port, I imagined the sheer force of will it must have taken to lay down these tracks. It was a will motivated by the enormous profits accruing from Sri Lankan tea and coffee and powered by indentured labor.

This is the origin story of every train track laid down in the nineteenth century. The first intercity railway line in the world was the Liverpool and Manchester Railway. While it would go on to become the first railway company to profit from passenger travel, it was not originally intended to carry travelers. It was a freight train carrying cotton from the port of Liverpool to Manchester, a quiet market town of weavers that had almost overnight become one of the biggest textile-manufacturing centers of Europe.

Cotton does not grow in Britain. The European infatuation with cotton began in India, in the South Indian city of

Kozhikode (which was mispronounced as Calicut), where they came across some plain-woven unbleached hand-loom cotton fabric. This fabric came to be known as calico. Kozhikode is where Vasco da Gama first made landfall in 1498, setting off a long chain of events that end with black pepper being available at grocery stores in Brooklyn, where I live now.

The beaches of Kozhikode are still lined with ware-houses. Along its famed mittayi theruvu, street of sweets, halwa makers and handloom shops sit side by side. It is the kind of old and unremarkable street that reminds you of old and unremarkable streets in Gaziantep and Harar. Streets that smell of generations of commerce, streets full of the forgotten possibility of a softer, gentler international trade. But that was before calico and chintz and muslin and bafta and gingham and chambray, named after the small places they were made in or the hyperlocal traditions they came out of, became raw materials for European capitalism.

To be clear, cotton had been a commodity of trade long before the arrival of the Europeans. The buying and selling of cotton was a big part of medieval Afro-Eurasian trade. In the old cotton system, writes Giorgio Riello, author of *Cotton: The Fabric that Made the Modern World*, cotton textiles percolated from the manufacturing hub in India across the Indian Ocean and trans-Saharan trade networks. It was the arrival of the European East Indian companies in India that restructured the system and scale of this trade. By the 1580s, the Portuguese were selling Indian cotton in North Africa and the Levant. An Indian cloth length sufficient to buy a slave in West Africa might cost twenty crusados, after which the same slave would be sold for five times as much in Brazil and eight times as much in the Caribbean and Mexican markets. Soon the Portuguese were joined by British, Dutch, and French traders. By transforming themselves from merchants to occupiers, they created the conditions that divided the world into First World and Third World. As Sven Beckert put it in *Empire of Cotton*, "Cotton from India, slaves from Africa, and sugar from the Caribbean moved across the planet in a complex commercial dance."

That long-ago eighteenth-century cotton-slavery nexus and its profits created a British middle class and made the United States one of the most prosperous nations in the world. It also ensured that African American descendants of the enslaved people did not partake of any of these profits. It erased many craft traditions in the Third World and riddled those countries with poverty, while enabling high levels of consumption and high-carbon lifestyles in Western Europe and the United States. Today, one cotton farmer in India commits suicide every eight hours. Generations of cyclical debt and poverty bear down on the living, as neocolonialism continues a trajectory of exploitation that began with European imperialism. "The shift of competitive advantage in cotton textiles from India to Britain was a key episode in the Great Divergence of living standards between Europe and Asia," write Stephen Broadberry and Bishnupriya Gupta, who study colonial economics. Cotton, one could say, is why people from many African and Asian countries have passports that need to show bank statements as "proof of income" when they apply for a visa to the United States or Western Europe.

Trains were instrumental to this process. The United States was an early adopter of trains, with Congress giving private railroad companies permission to build railway tracks on land that belonged to various Indigenous nations. In *Empire's Tracks: Indigenous Nations, Chinese Workers, and the Transcontinental Railroad*, Manu Karuka writes of how the government also sent its soldiers to protect the railroads. The annals of railroad building in the United States are full of stories of soldiers and railroad engineers defending the tracks and trains against various tribal attacks—in fact, the Pawnee and the Sioux and the Blackfoot and other Indigenous communities that gained a reputation for their warlike tendencies were merely resisting the illegal encroachment on their treaty-protected hunting grounds by railroad investors. The railway line that runs between Chicago and Seattle is still called the Empire Builder. Around the world, trains were empire builders.

It did not surprise me to find out that the Indian railways were built to transport cotton and other raw materials and to fortify British military outposts. What did surprise me was learning how Indian railway building was funded. I was under the impression that the Indian railways were a public works project, funded by the empire. In reality, though, the Indian railway-building project was a story of private enterprise funded by public funds. As in the case of the Manchester line, the initial impetus for building railways in India came from merchants in London who had their eye on easier access to raw cotton from India. The private investors behind railway companies persuaded the East India Company and later the British government in India to offset the risk of their investments through a system of economic guarantees wherein the government taxed its Indian subjects to make up the difference between real and projected profits. In other words, the Indian railways were funded by the British government in the same way that Donald Trump is a self-made millionaire.

This is the world that Phileas Fogg circumnavigates in *Around the World in Eighty Days*. Rereading the book now, I find it littered with clues about this frenetic colonial-capitalist plunder.

Francis Cromarty, a military officer whom Fogg's party travels with in India, is on his way to Banaras to join his troops, which are encamped outside that city. Aouda, a young Parsi widow that Fogg's party dramatically rescues from burning in her dead husband's pyre, is from a family of cotton merchants. When Fogg's party takes the train across the United States, the train they are traveling in is attacked by the Sioux. In the foreground of the book, we have the eccentric British gentleman whose determination and resourcefulness help him travel the world in eighty days. In the background, the crackdown on India after the Rebellion of 1857, the rapacious cotton colonialism, the rescue of women as a pretext for colonial interference, the westward expansion of the U.S. military state, the takeover of Indigenous lands, and how all this is powered by a depleting supply of fossil fuels that will lead to more and more planetary destruction. On the final lap of his journey, after he has missed the transatlantic liner that will take him from New York back to England, Fogg hires a trading ship whose captain agrees to take him to France. As soon as he gets on the ship, Fogg promptly bribes the crew and takes the captain hostage and sets the ship sailing for England. Toward the end of this voyage, the coal supply runs low. Unwittingly foreshadowing climate change, Fogg starts burning the wood in the very frame of the ship he is traveling in so that he can keep it moving to reach England in eighty days.

Of course, ten-year-old me, jolting along in a familiar blue train that smelled of diesel and chai and stopped for imagined gold-chain robbers, did not know all this. So even as I was skeptical of Fogg's faith in the punctuality of trains, I marveled at the cool confidence with which Phileas Fogg expected to travel around the world in eighty days. Even his friends at the Reform Club didn't think it possible, hence the wager. But even in their incredulity, there is entitlement. As Lord Albemarle says: "If the thing is feasible, the first to do it ought to be an Englishman."

Fogg's confidence and nonchalance in the face of adversity is something Jules Verne presents as an extraordinary personality trait. But Fogg is simply a product of his time and place. Self-confidence was the Victorians' chief characteristic, as James Munson and Richard Mullen put it in *The Smell of the Continent: The British Discover Europe*. British tourists were armed with the belief that their country was the most important one in the world. In this and other matters, this fictional story about one man's epic quest to circumnavigate the world by train and steamer is actually a nonfiction history of how an empire furnishes its citizens with the possibility of travel and how such travel, with its individualistic and heroic overtones, subtly reinforces the empire. Fogg's confidence in himself is actually his trust in the empire. British wanderlust was financed and operationalized by the colonies.

Strictly speaking, wanderlust is not an object, like cotton is. And yet, to me, wanderlust is material. Wanderlust is an act of consumption. The $8 trillion tourism industry has become adept at dressing it up as a dream, a feeling, a natural instinct, when, in fact, wanderlust is made possible by colonialism and capitalism. Eighteenth-century colonialism gave us Wanderlust 1.0, and twentieth-century capitalism gave us Wanderlust 2.0, and now here we are, poised on the verge of yet another software update to wanderlust.

This is why wanderlust frequently attaches itself to advertising copy for objects that do not have any connection to wandering. As twenty-first-century consumers, our imagination has been trained to be tempted by these intertextual cross-cultural references even when we don't fully understand them. So of course we get it—wanderlust in a credit card ad is referring to a certain kind of luxury travel; wanderlust in a coffee ad is suggesting how your favorite beverage came to you from far away and thereby drinking it is an act of travel; wanderlust in a clothing ad is painting a vision of how these clothes can renew you as if you were traveling. This is one of my hobbies: decoding #wanderlust in advertising copy.

My favorite example of this is the Indian designer Sabyasachi's 2021 "Wanderlust" collection for H&M. The collection featured the kind of gauzy floral block prints and flowy fabrics that are considered ethnic clothing on women of color and resort wear on white women. "I am a nomad at heart," Sabyasachi said in an interview with *Vogue India*, describing how the collection, "aimed at the millennials who love adventure and glamping," offers customers a vision of the travel that they missed so much during the pandemic. The aesthetic is generally bohemian, with tons of loose fabric and layers of jangling jewelry and a general air of idleness. But the romance underpinning this hinges on what the cultural critic Paromita Vohra called the "iconography of tropical colonialism"—heat, dust, and pale, gaunt models on verandas and in gardens that suggest, without showing, silent servants to bring cold drinks.

I came across another intriguing example of wanderlust haymaking while sunshining in a 2021 press release from the Four Seasons hotel group:

> After a year of lockdowns and restrictions, it's clear that travel is more than just a "nice to have": it's an essential part of life for many. Now, as vacations and getaways become less of a dream and more of a possibility, travelers can finally shift from wanderlust—the longing to travel—to wandermust, the insatiable need to travel."

This is indeed the key to modern wanderlust: its insatiability. And it is not the insatiability of curiosity. It is the insatiability of consumption. As sociologist Colin Campbell wrote, modern consumption is less about satisfying a want and more about finding the next want.. "No sooner is one satisfied than another is waiting in line clamoring to be satisfied; when this one is attended to, another appears, then subsequently a fourth and so on, apparently without end . . . How is it possible for wants to appear with such constancy, and in such an inexhaustible fashion?" he asks, and I feel the despair in the question. I want to take a moment and sit down with this question, and I will do it, right after I finish planning my summer travels. I have to research airfares, click through hundreds of Instagram posts, read hotel reviews. I have to buy a new suitcase.

We, the moderns, travel not because we have wanderlust but because we can have wanderlust. It doesn't bubble up from the wild pockets of humanness deep inside our souls; rather, it is programmed into the suggestible material of our consciousness by the media we are surrounded by, whether it is Wordsworth's poetry or that Instagram influencer pulling her boyfriend into the frame in front of Saint Mark's Basilica in Venice one week and a beach in Bali a few weeks later.

•

During those long overnight train rides of my childhood, sitting in my second-class compartment, I often wondered about the first-class compartments. What did the air-conditioning feel like? Were the seats softer? Were the toilets cleaner? It was like thinking about a foreign country. It rarely occurred to me to wonder about the general class, which is the cheapest and hence poorest class of travel in Indian trains. When I did think of the people in those compartments, I felt a vague kindness. *Those poor people. I hope it's not too bad for them.* Then my thoughts would wander again toward the air-conditioned first-class compartments. Did they get better food in there? Were their cutlets crisper? Was their coffee less watery?

Regardless of the class of travel, many Indian trains discharge human waste on the rails. This poses an unsightly problem, considering 23 million passengers ride around twelve thousand Indian trains daily. The problem has been solved thus far by using manual scavengers. Note the passive voice. The Indian railways categorically state that they do not employ humans to remove excrement and rubbish from the tracks. Manual scavenging is prohibited in India, especially since it has been associated with caste oppression. Yet the feces on the tracks continue to be carted away by human beings using brooms. In *Unseen: The Truth About Manual Scavenging*, Bhasha Singh writes about how the railways get away with this by simply not acknowledging the sanitation workers as their employees. Instead they outsource the cleaning to the contractors, who employ sanitation workers, most of them drawn from the most oppressed castes. The capitalist logic of outsourcing work thus enables the feudal logic of caste oppression.

The coffee was just as watery, I found out after graduating

into first-class compartments occasionally as an upwardly mobile adult. The creature comforts were just slightly better. But what I was paying for now was not so much comfort as insulation. The first-class compartments insulate those who are traveling in them from crowds, the noise and smells of those crowds, the frustration of crowds and the frustration of being part of a crowd. Briefly we can pretend to live in a world that is not bursting at the seams with needs, a world where the means and ends are in the right proportion. Perhaps this is the underlying premise of luxury—to not see other people's needs.

•

From the beginning, trains were a site of class anxiety. Early British trains offered three different classes of travel, and the third class was an open boxcar until 1844, when the British parliament laid down a law that third-class travelers must be sheltered from the elements and provided with seats. When we think of vintage train travel, we usually think of the Orient Express, but it was that bare-bones third-class seat, costing a penny per mile, that propelled tourism into a mass market phenomenon. Thus, while they were enabling imperial enrichment, trains were also democratizing travel. In this, they represent the contradictions at the heart of so much tourism. As mid-nineteenth-century labor legislation compelled employers to make half Saturdays and Sundays holidays, it was trains that made it possible for European factory workers to participate in the possibilities of leisure: the day trip to the beach, team sports, and, of course, the packaged tour. I do not have any evidence for this, but "So what are you doing this weekend?," the question dreaded by introverts everywhere, probably has its provenance around this time.

The packaged tour was the brainchild of a Baptist minister, Thomas Cook, whose original mission was to rid the world of alcoholism. The first Cook's Tour, in which he took 570 passengers on a one-day rail excursion on July 5, 1841, was to a temperance rally with anti-drink speakers and bands. It might seem like a funny coincidence that nineteenth century's most famous travel agent began as a temperance evangelist. So much of tourism history is about these funny coincidences that turn out to be subterranean socioeconomic interlinkages. The working-class tourist excursion was a solution to a question that vexed English policymakers and social reformers deeply in the middle of the nineteenth century. In *The Tourist Gaze*, John Urry writes that as work came to be organized as a relatively time-bound and space-bound activity separate from play, religion, and festivity, it became necessary to invent rational recreation. As the idle poor were converted into working classes, it became necessary to give them opportunities for well-behaved leisure. Thomas Cook's first temperance tour was an attempt at this. Its success motivated him to offer more ambitious vacation packages. In 1845, he organized a trip to Scotland. Everything that could go wrong went wrong. There were no toilets on the train, tea was promised but never appeared, and, on the way to Scotland, the steamship ran into a storm. The passengers, who had each paid fourteen shillings, were

wet, hungry, and tired. It was magnificent. And mass tourism was born.

I thought of those first tourists when I came across an
April 2011 article in *The New Yorker* in which Evan Osnos
treated himself to the "Classic European," an all-inclusive
Chinese packaged tour that would cover five countries in
ten days. Osnos is the only non-Chinese person on the
tour, and over the course of the article, we meet his Chinese traveling companions and see their responses to Europe, the suburban hotels they stay in to save money, the
windowless-basement Chinese restaurant in Paris where
they eat lunch, the Chinese-language welcome cards they
receive at the department store Galeries Lafayette "promising happiness, longevity, and a ten-per-cent discount," in
a mysterious place called Aotelaise that Osnos eventually
decodes as "outlets."

For years, this article stayed with me, with its casually
mocking descriptions of the Chinese tourists traveling
outside their country. Early on, while flying to Frankfurt,
Osnos opens his packet of "Outbound Group Advice."
The tour members are discouraged from giving money to
"Gypsies begging beside the road." Someone asking for
help taking a photo could be a con artist. "I'd been in and
out of Europe over the years, but the instructions put it
in a new light, and I was oddly reassured to be travelling
with three dozen others and a guide," Osnos says, slyly setting his own worldliness against the naivete of the Chinese tourists. They represent a new vanguard of Chinese
travel, after decades of Communist suspicion of tourism,

he informs the reader. About China's remarkable medieval history of maritime inventors and navigators and diplomats and adventurous Buddhist pilgrims, Osnos has one sentence: "Zheng He, a fifteenth-century eunuch, famously sailed the emperor's fleet as far as Africa, to 'set eyes on barbarian regions.'"

At one point, the Chinese guide tells the tourists: "In China, we think of bus drivers as superhumans who can work twenty-four hours straight, no matter how late we want them to drive. But in Europe, unless there's weather or traffic, they're only allowed to drive for twelve hours!" I knew that the guide must have said this. I knew that sentence must have gone through *The New Yorker*'s rigorous fact-checking process. So why did that exclamation mark at the end of that sentence feel so wrong? That exclamation mark was making fun of the traveler from the developing country, wide-eyed and awestruck, not by European culture and history but by the human rights of bus drivers.

While the Chinese tourists are busy seeing the sights of Europe, the Chinese tourists are the "sights" that Osnos is seeing. Each tourist emerges as a type symbolizing something Chinese and nouveau riche, from the frugal couple who kept track of exactly how much the group had spent on each bottle of water to the teenager who asks Osnos if the American constitution prevents private companies from getting government support. Readers are supposed to be marveling at the small-mindedness of the tourists, but instead I found myself marveling at the nouveau-Orientalism of the article. It illustrates so thoroughly what Debbie Lisle in *The Global Politics of Contemporary Travel Writing* calls contemporary travel writing's participation in the anxieties created by globalization. Lisle astutely observes that contemporary travel writing often alleviates these anxieties by reproducing the logic of a colonial vision, *but in a cosmopolitan guise*. This is not an unreconstructed version of Orientalism, Lisle notes, because contemporary travel writers know enough to frame their encounters with others in positive ways, revealing moments of empathy and recognition of difference, realizations of equality. However, the cosmopolitan vision is firmly undergirded by the colonial vision of an enlightened and superior western traveler constructing an inferior "other" in order to justify the continuation of hierarchical global relations.

In 2019, the year that the Thomas Cook travel agency declared bankruptcy abruptly in September, leaving about 150,000 British travelers stranded around the globe, the number of outbound tourists from China reached nearly 163 million. Prior to Covid-19's upending travel routines, Chinese travelers had surpassed U.S. tourist spending and were only slightly behind in terms of volume: for comparison, in 2018, U.S. travelers took 157,873,000 trips abroad, with each tourist spending an average of $1,155, while Chinese tourists took 154,632,000 trips abroad, spending $1,794 per capita. Little wonder then that many tourist sites in Europe are adding Mandarin audio guides to their offerings while upmarket department stores such as Galeries Lafayette and Printemps are frantically wooing Chinese tourists with store maps in Chinese and Chinese-speaking store attendants.

In the changing landscape of contemporary tourism, poking fun at Chinese tourists is about as useful as searching for an authentic curry. These ships have sailed long ago—literally and metaphorically. We are all tourists now, those of us who describe ourselves as travelers and nomads and vagrants the more so because it simply means we have bought into the ultimate tourist myth, that we can escape tourism and simply travel.

A few years ago, my husband and I were walking around Barcelona when we got a hankering for Thai food. Even now, I feel a twinge of embarrassment to be admitting this, but there we were. After two weeks wandering around Spain eating tortilla de papas, after a delightfully comic afternoon when we had racked our brains to ask for hot sauce in Spanish and were offered a tureen of warm gravy, after encountering gazpacho's charming cousin salmorejo, after all that—we had the hubris to be bored. To think, *Wouldn't it be nice to dig into a big garlicky bowl of noodles, laced with lemongrass and soy sauce?* So we looked up Thai restaurants on our phones and made for the nearest one: a business-like little restaurant on a side street in the touristy district. Inside, the restaurant was all tourists like us, slightly shamefaced, as if Anthony Bourdain could see us all and was shaking his head in disgust. The menu spelled out in English the usual suspects: the various pads, the curries in primary and secondary colors. But toward the back of the restaurant was a doorway that, strangely enough, led to the restaurant next door. And the aromas coming through that doorway were familiar and enticing. We walked through and found ourselves in an Indian restaurant, but unlike the Thai restaurant, it clearly knew what it was doing. We decided to put away our Thai food hankerings and ate excellent dal and aloo gobi for lunch.

After I paid our bill to the Indian man who sat behind the cash counter, after he and I compared our different migration paths and checked if we knew anyone in common among the 1 billion people back home, I asked him about the Thai restaurant he was running next door. "Oh, that," he said. "It's for Americans. Thai food very popular with them."

He had seen us coming before we even got our hankerings. He knew that he could count on enough tourists from the United States to get bored with Spanish food and hanker for Thai food. And we had obliged. We had been programmed by the algorithm of our life in Brooklyn, where Thai restaurants dot the landscape liberally and we look forward to our weekly pad kee mao. Like Pavlov's dog, we developed a craving for Thai food exactly ten days, three hours, forty minutes, and six seconds into our travels in Spain. *Hmmm*, we would think, from the eternal sunshine of the spotless American tourist mind, *how strange, but I seem to be wanting a big garlicky bowl of noodles, laced with lemongrass and soy sauce.*

On the surface, the backstory of a moment like this contains two obvious strands: the South Asian entrepreneurial migration and the abundance of "ethnic" foods from around the globe in the United States. But there's at least one more surprising strand braided into this hybridity. In

2002, the Thai government launched a program of culinary diplomacy aimed at increasing the number of Thai restaurants around the world. Over the course of the next decade, the number of Thai restaurants in First World countries such as the United States, New Zealand, and Australia rose exponentially as the Thai government trained thousands of chefs, offered loans to Thai nationals who wanted to start restaurants, and published a training manual on catering to foreign taste buds. The aim was simply to popularize dishes such as pad thai and pad see ew. The program was based on an astute calculation that these dishes would in turn inspire tourism to Thailand—the calculation paid off, and Thailand increasingly became a major tourist destination, leaving neighboring countries well behind in number of visitors.

When I think of my favorite travel moments, I often return to this scene. Of course, a deep state conspiracy to feed me pad kee mao is delightful in itself, but what is especially delicious is all the sweet and sour ironies of the moment. Finally, travel had paid off in an epiphany, and the epiphany was that I was a cliché. A tourist. How bracing it is to catch a glimpse of the software that is running me and hundreds of thousands of others, silently and efficiently humming away beneath the surface of our wanderlust. And equally, how invigorating to encounter the multiple hybridities of this place we call the twenty-first century.

Chapter

EIGHT

✈

I GREW UP AMID OTHER PEOPLE'S VACATIONS. BEACHES, mountains, culture: Kerala has the classic trifecta of modern tourism. Travel writers have a hard time writing about Kerala and its tranquil rivers and manicured tea estates and golden beaches without using the word *lush*. Over the course of my childhood, Kerala cleverly disguised itself as a tourist paradise, a place where people discovered themselves anew while cruising in a houseboat or wandering through a spice plantation.

I did not grow up skipping down lush green plantation trails. In fact, that was the childhood my parents happily left behind, moving out of their villages in the hills of Kerala to set up home in the hustle and bustle and tussle of Ernakulam, a seaside city. There was nothing lush about Ernakulam. My parents embraced urban living with enthusiasm. Two train stations! Hospitals! Schools! My siblings and I were urban children; we knew how to clamber onto Ernakulam's breakneck-fast buses. We attended a school where a tiny lawn was the only patch of green. We grew up on the sidelines of Ernakulam's never-ending development, apartment towers stacking up precariously while the city

ticked off construction megaprojects: an international airport, overpasses, a new metro system. For me, Kerala was
Mahatma Gandhi Road, with its speeding buses and glitzy
sari shops, restaurants full of loud conversation, the sound
of the vaanku merging with chants from a Hindu temple.
"What's your native place?" adults would often ask one another, because so many of that generation had moved from
their native villages to cities, in search of the promises of
modernity.

So I learned to think of nature as something you left behind. My eyes were trained on bigger cities as I grew up.
Since then, I have lived in Delhi, New York, and Istanbul:
all cities with layers of history and fierce neighborhood cultures. A few years ago, I stayed with some writer friends in
a mountain village in southern France. Other than Wed-
nesdays, when a grocery truck visited, and monthly hunting
days, when local hunters took to the mountains and then
brought their spoils to the village square, the village was
silent and peaceful. After two months in this village, I took
a train to Madrid, arriving late in the night at a friend's
apartment. Early the next morning, I woke up and went to
the window to look out at the street that was coming to life.
Someone was walking their dog and someone else was going home after a night binge. I watched them almost collide, step aside, collide again, smile ruefully at each other.
Watching from a second-floor window, I felt moved, nour-
ished, revived. Cities, weird, wonderful cities, where strangers come together to make meaning out of collisions. How
I love cities.

Nature, though, has always confounded me. For a long time, the urban park was about as natural as I wanted. When I came across rapturous descriptions of nature in books, my eyes skimmed over the paragraphs. Even just hearing about camping makes me want to take a hot shower. I have a city-dweller's deep distrust of any place without sidewalks and air-conditioning and coffee makers. Plus, nature has snakes.

There's a story in the Mahabharata about King Parikshit. While hunting in a forest, he gets lost and asks a sanyasi for directions. But the sanyasi is meditating and does not answer. So in a fit of impatience, King Parikshit throws a dead snake on the sanyasi. When the sanyasi's son sees this, he curses King Parikshit to die of snakebite in seven days. The king fortifies his life against snakes and spends the next week at the top of a tower guarded by soldiers who are instructed to kill every snake they see. For seven days, the king's priests chant prayers for his long life. As the seventh day winds to a close, the king reaches for a plum in a fruit basket and takes a bite. There is a tiny worm in the fruit. It immediately grows into Takshaka, King of Snakes, who kills Parikshit with a swift bite.

Ever since I read the story as a child, I have been wary of snakes. Having never flung a dead snake on a meditating sanyasi while out hunting, there is zero reason for me to worry so much. But I do. The Mahabharata is full of devastation, from bloody battles to apocalyptic floods, but the worm in the plum fruit has always been my favorite personal metaphor for utter devastation. It is climate change and nuclear annihilation, rolled into one intimate moment. It is walls with lead and roofs with asbestos, endocrine disruptors in toothpaste, microplastic in drinking water. Nothing is safe, not even a pasture-raised grass-fed organic fruit, served to a king on top of a tower.

So yes, I am terrified of snakes. Even writing the word *snake* makes my toes curl. Under every bush in nature, I am convinced, there are snakes. And people keep telling me stories of their snake encounters—a friend who had a craft store in a village in India told me that in the rainy season, snakes would crawl into her shop and cozy up inside swaths of fabric. Another friend who lives in the outback in Australia told me that she has to turn her boots upside down before she wears them, lest a desert snake has crept in during the night. These friends don't know, but my brain has filed away these stories very carefully, and anytime I am not in a city, I am bracing myself to see Takshaka, King of Snakes, waiting for me: in a basket of fruit, in a toilet bowl, under a bed.

•

A few years ago, I was visiting an ashram in India with my daughter and husband. My husband, a journalist who was then writing about illegal sand mining in rivers, was interviewing a sanyasi who had become a river activist. As they talked, our daughter, then four years old, wandered off and sat down on the riverbank and started drawing in the clay with a twig. The swami looked at her and said, "Whenever a child comes to visit the ashram, this is what happens.

They start playing with the mud. Children are immediately drawn to the earth."

His simple observation went through me like a knife. What parent has not noticed that specific happiness that comes upon a child let loose in nature? Watching my daughter scramble around in parks and backyards, dancing in the mud and reveling in puddles, reminded me that a long time ago, I, too, knew how to take pleasure in mud and twigs and crunchy fallen leaves and logs and fast-flowing streams. It's not just that children love nature. Children are nature. In the spontaneous joy they get from the earth and water and trees, there is a reminder of ancient animal impulses that we all carry within us. What had happened to me? Why did wilderness feel fearful to me? I started wondering then if my love for cities, at least partly, had something more sinister underneath it.

Fear of nature, known as biophobia, is a real phenomenon in our increasingly urban world. We spend most of our lives in buildings and vehicles, our leisure time is largely taken up by screens, and our environments have been denatured. Richard Louv, writing about how children suffer from the broken bond between them and nature, refers to "nature deficit." As I sat there in the ashram with birdsong in my ear, world leaders were meeting to negotiate a climate-change agreement. It was easy enough to connect the dotted line between my own biophobia and the reluctance of powerful men and women to make amends for what we as a species have done. If birds and trees and rivers could sign documents, we would have stopped climate change in its tracks a long time ago. But humans, increasingly urban around the world, seem to have forgotten that we too are nature. The wilderness strikes fear in so many of us, and why would we want to be good stewards of what we fear? As glaciers melt and plastic piles up at the bottom of our oceans, I started wondering if my aversion to nature was actually a version of the banality of evil.

•

"You have to be very lucky to see a snake," Sam said to me. "They are shy." I was pulling on long gum boots to wear for a hike in the forest. Sam is the resident guide at a small guesthouse, set deep inside a forest in Wayanad, in the northern hills of Kerala. I had told Sam that I was afraid of snakes, and he was reassuring me that I probably wouldn't see one. He should have stopped there, but he didn't.

"Funny incident a few years ago. Two men were riding a motorbike down the mountain when they saw an eagle flying off with a cobra. But the snake was struggling so much the eagle dropped it, right on top of the passenger on the motorbike. Crazy, alle? The snake was so confused, of course, it bit the man. In the neck. He died. Poor man."

In the Indian epics, the forest is where princes are unfairly exiled, usually for twelve years. Determined to make amends for my nature deficit, I was exiling myself to a forest, for a mere twelve days. Wayanad, with its fierce mountains and silent forests, had sounded like a perfect destination to immerse in nature. The guesthouse we were in, sitting two thousand meters above sea level, used to be the home of a

British settler who cultivated spices on about five hundred acres. Now it bears little resemblance to a plantation; the new owners have allowed nature to take its course, and the forest has reclaimed the neat slopes where cardamom plants and pepper vines once grew. Dense clusters of ferns flourished in the shade of towering trees.

The guesthouse has a minimal footprint; it is staffed by preservationists and local Indigenous people, and all the profits go into taking care of the forest. There was only one road up the mountain, and we had been driven up in a semi-open Jeep while pouring rain soaked us and made the rocky road even more perilous. Now we were deep inside the forest, in an old house built on a clearing perched on top of the mountain. Clouds floated past the veranda, and trees covered every inch of the surrounding mountains like moss on rocks.

And here, dear reader, we have reached the limits of my ability to describe nature. Having skimmed all those nature descriptions in books means that nature will always be an impressionist painting for me. There are writers who can tell you about different leaf shapes and name the many trees that dotted these mountains. Unfortunately I will not be able to do that. Incoherence bubbles up inside me, choking me off. All I can tell you is that I was surrounded by mesmerizing shades of blue and green.

But the air. Let me try to tell you about the air. Air as cold and sweet as ice cream. Air so rich my poor, sad lungs, fed on smoke and exhaust and mold, felt like thieves to be breathing it so freely. Air so delicious that I finally understood why breathing, just breathing, could be a joy. Air that went hand in hand with the rich, deep silence of the mountain. I cannot believe that there was a time when all air was like this.

Of course, it is a dangerous fantasy to think that the past is a perfect place. It is especially dangerous in the context of postcolonial thought, because it is all too easy to romanticize a precolonial Edenic version, as if all evil, from racism to environmental degradation, were introduced by the colonizers. Kerala had been doing a terrific job at propagating caste and class inequities before the colonizers arrived, one after the other. But until British colonial rulers systematically razed forests to plant tea, teak, coffee, and spices, Kerala, like the rest of India, was mostly wilderness. The environmental activist Madhav Gadgil writes of how early British travelers described India as an ocean of trees. The colonial state appropriated virtually all forests, supposedly to manage them in an enlightened and scientific fashion. Taking forests away from the many communities that lived in them and near them and took care of them, they razed entire forests to the ground to facilitate the harvesting of timber and to facilitate plantation agriculture, substantially depleting forest cover by 1860. Postindependence India has largely continued this tradition, including the encroachment of tribal lands.

It would never have occurred to my parents to take us to a wilderness destination on a holiday. The few times we went on holiday, we took those long train rides to the big cities that enamored us. Monuments, shopping, eating out: this was our idea of a vacation worth spending money on. Besides, we had our native places: the villages my parents grew up in, still thrillingly (for children) and exasperatingly (for parents) remote and tree-covered in the 1990s. When we visited my grandmother's village in those days, we had to take a train to the nearest town, catch a bus from there, then wait for an uncle or cousin to pick us up in a bone-rattling Jeep. I dreaded that final ride because the twisted mountain roads would make me throw up. Still, the first sight of the river, which I thought of as my grandmother's river, would bring relief and comfort and the promise of jackfruit chips. Those villages had rapidly turned into small towns, and now my grandmother's house on the river was next to a bridge that brought buses and trucks to her doorstep. My grandmother herself was no more, and the house was slowly crumbling.

My grandmother would have loved that bridge. Having spent a lifetime enduring weeklong power outages and racing against the local fox to scoop up chicken eggs, she would have welcomed all that it made possible—groceries trucked in, plumbers and electricians who could bike across from town, not being cut off when the river was flooded. The bridge was universally considered a blessing: even as it was being built, on my extended-family WhatsApp group, we watched it grow as if it were a fetus. Now that it straddles the river, we keep tabs on it from around the world, especially during the monsoons when the waters rise. The older generations in that WhatsApp group boast about having had to swim across the river to go to school. Now the bridge has opened up an array of schools and colleges as options for the young people of the village. It has spurred the local economy and made village life much more spontaneous. Yet something was lost too. And now all over India, parents like me are seeking out wilderness destinations for our children and ourselves. Every big city in India is now surrounded by a belt of getaways as more and more urban dwellers, exhausted by the daily grind that makes our lives convenient and comfortable, seek refuge in nature.

There are parallels here to the way the Industrial Revolution in England made tourism necessary and possible. But did that generation of tourists live with a quietly ticking clock counting the days down to the final glacier? The way we seek out nature now is tinged with mourning and alarm, and every time I looked out at the thick forests that covered the mountains in Wayanad, I felt the sad dilemma of being human in the twenty-first century. Reviewing Barry Lopez's *Horizon*, Rachel Riederer wrote about how for a previous generation of travelers, traveling into nature was an absolute good, "undertaken without this modern anxiety." From our perspective as inheritors and co-creators of a fully formed climate crisis, Lopez's lifetime of wandering is a chronicle of ultimate luxury, she concludes. There's also a genre of nature travel that is "last-chance tourism"—visiting places that will never be the same again or are about to disappear forever. But isn't that basically every place on earth, sooner or later? Someday, I knew, Kerala would disappear. Sandwiched between the Arabian Sea and the Western Ghats, with low-lying backwaters already prone to floods, what chance did it have against rising sea levels?

Unfortunately, underneath the pain and anxiety I feel about all this, there is a layer of smugness I can't seem to escape from—what a good person I was for caring, for having these high-flown thoughts about nature, despite what modernity had done to me. And beneath the smugness, a constant flow of irritation toward the leeches.

"Congratulations," the irrepressible Sam said when he noticed me, within an hour of our arrival, trying to pick a couple of leeches off my elbow. According to him, the little bloodsuckers will purify your blood, so you're lucky to have them. Just like you are lucky to see snakes, I suppose. Sam showed me how to get the leeches off with a salt stick (a bundle of salt wrapped in cloth and tied to the bottom of a stick). Clawing them off one's skin does little; they simply leave some teeth in your flesh. Leeches are a fact of life during the monsoon in Kerala. When it rains relentlessly, they emerge from water bodies and start making their way up any warm bodies in the vicinity.

Every day we went for long hikes in the forest, equipped with salt sticks and nylon leech socks and gum boots. Every day we came back with leeches crawling all over us. Leeches find their way by sensing heat. Groping their way toward warmth, they make their way up animal flesh and press their three hundred tiny claws into skin to start sucking blood and sustenance. Soon I got so tired of trying to get them off me that I only picked off the most persistent ones. I got used to patches of blood leaking out of my body.

Sam's love for the forest was infectious. "Elephants always stop to snack on this fruit tree," he would say. Or "This is where the bison come to drink water." Once, he picked up what looked like a twig and showed us that it was the needle of a hedgehog. The week before we arrived, he said, he had to wait for a tiger sleeping on the road to wake up and saunter into the forest before he could drive on. After a point, these stories started to feel mythical. Our hikes through the forest were always beautiful, but we never had any animal sightings that I can boast about. Except maybe one day when a little green snake slithered past us before I had the time to get afraid. "Very poisonous snake," Sam said, looking at its tail fondly as it disappeared into the undergrowth. "Two or three minutes you would be dead if it bit you." At one point he stopped and sniffed the air. "I smell tiger," he said. I sniffed the air. Nothing. It was as if Sam had another set of senses. He had walked the land alone a thousand times. The forest was a book or rather a library full of books, and he was a scholar steeped in the study of it. Whereas I was forest illiterate.

One day Sam stopped to show us tiger scratch marks on a tree trunk. A few moments later, he showed us an animal skeleton that lay in a clearing. It was a baby elephant, he told us, likely killed by the tiger that then ate the elephant over the course of several days. The rain-washed white bones lay starkly on grass that still showed evidence of the animal's fight. They looked like signs, and as I pieced them together—ribs, mud, bloodstained leaves—I felt like a toddler learning to read. On another hike, we heard a brusque percussive sound. It was sambar deer calling in the forest to alert other deer. A tiger was probably on the prowl, Sam calmly interpreted. Shouldn't we return? I asked. "It's nowhere near us," he said. "If you see a tiger, the best thing to do is to raise your hands as high as you can, exaggerate your size, and make lots of noise," he told me. "You have to be very lucky to see a tiger."

He also seemed to have misunderstood my fear of snakes as a form of curiosity. Pretty much any innocent conversation with Sam degenerated into him whipping out his cell phone to show me pictures of snakes. Snakes snakes snakes! Snakes with gleaming black skin and yellow spots, snakes that looked like purple garden hoses, snakes that looked mildly taken aback to be photographed. Then one day, amid the barrage of snake photos, I saw a picture of a young woman with long black hair holding a smiling toddler on her hips. "Oh, that's my wife," he said, quickly moving past that one. Wait, wait, I wanted to know more. Sam's wife and son lived in a town three hours away, because, schools and hospitals. The same reason my own parents had scrambled out of the villages they grew up in. There was one rocky cliff near a waterfall in the forest where, magically, sometimes we would find cell phone reception. Sometimes on our hikes, Sam led us there, and the three of us would all fall on our phones eagerly. And Sam would download photos of his son growing up without him. It was his wife's labor as a mostly solo parent that made it possible for Sam to work his dream job.

One day he showed me a picture in which he was "playing" with a baby cobra. When he saw my face blanch, he told me that cobras are far less dangerous than the Russell's viper, a snake common in Wayanad. A cobra at least warns you with a hissing sound; the viper just makes its stabbing attack unceremoniously. Its jaws are strong enough to take out a chunk of flesh, but it also delivers deadly venom.

"Many people have been killed by this snake," he said with a kind of grudging admiration as I used my salt stick to tap leeches off me. You have to be very lucky to die like this, I could imagine him saying next.

We had such different ideas of danger. I have spent all my life trying not to be attacked. This sounds melodramatic if you are not a woman. But for women, the danger of wilderness is not just about encountering wild animals or slipping and falling into the rapids; it is also the danger posed by men. Even in the well-marked urban park outside my apartment building in New York City, I would never venture to be alone after a certain time of the night. There are paths I would never take in that park alone during daytime. During the pandemic, there was a string of attempted rapes in the park. For days after that, I could not bring myself to venture to the park for a walk, even during the day. The specter of violence follows women everywhere, and it walks out with us into the great outdoors. At least in part, my biophobia is also androphobia. So much of nature writing frames nature as an alternative space, an antidote to all the oppressions and distractions of built spaces. A place where we can tune back into our inner noble savage frequencies. In fact, who we are in built spaces is who we are in nature. How could it be otherwise?

In an essay titled "Black Women and the Wilderness," Evelyn White writes of reckoning with her fear of nature during a visit to the Cascade Mountains of Oregon. "While the river's roar gave me a certain comfort and my heart warmed when I gazed at the sun-dappled trees outside a classroom window, I didn't want to get closer," she wrote. "I was certain that if I

ventured outside to admire a meadow or to feel the cool rip-
ples in a stream, I would be taunted, attacked, raped, maybe
even murdered because of the color of my skin." The anxiety
women feel in nature has additional layers for Black women,
for other women of color, for queer women, for trans women,
for women with disabilities—and none of it is because of
snakes or slippery waterways. It is because the wilderness,
too, has become a space where male privilege plays out. From
hunting to natural science to wilderness tourism, men have
claimed the landscape of wilderness and the metaphors of its
ruggedness. The framing of wilderness as the antithesis of do-
mesticity, of rule of law, of safety, has served men so well.

•

"Did you see anything?" another guest asked me when I returned to the guesthouse one day after a hike. "No, I did
not," I replied. Which was not true. I had seen trees and
plants and bushes; I had seen butterflies and mynahs and, of
course, leeches. But we both knew what she meant—did you
see any magnificent wild animals? I felt embarrassed that I
had nothing to show for my exertions.

So much of nature tourism has become premised on the
idea of the animal as spectacle. All over the world today,
there are animal sanctuaries and even big-game parks that
allow visitors to not just see but also touch, hug, take photos of, and interact with exotic animal species. But the idea
of a sanctuary where you can interact with animals is an
oxymoron. In many tourism-hungry places, there is also a

tendency to slap words like *sanctuary* and *refuge* even on places that parade animals cruelly.

Natasha Daly reporting for *National Geographic* wrote about two different elephant sites in Thailand, not too far from each other. The first one is famous for an elephant that can paint. Meena the elephant is so good at painting that she can paint an elephant in the wild, which is then sold to tourists. Meena spends her days and nights in chains, and, because she has a kicking problem, her trainer has put one of her feet in a spiked ring so that she cannot rest that foot. Nearby is the Elephant EcoValley, where there are no performing elephants like Meena. Instead, tourists can watch elephants bathe in the river and buy paper made of elephant dung. Daly writes that it's the kind of place where a visitor can feel a bit superior. But the same company runs both places and uses the same elephants. Elephant EcoValley simply targets tourists who would prefer not to see the animals suffering in plain sight. This is such a sadly apt metaphor for the way captive-wildlife tourism has become adept at catering to our fantasies—not just of interacting with animals but of ourselves as compassionate people.

At the heart of conventional conservation is the model of the American national park. The Indian environmentalist Madhav Gadgil writes of the influence of the top-down strategy modeled on Yosemite National Park, whose establishment in 1890 followed the forcible expulsion of the Native Americans who lived there. The history of "America's best idea" goes hand in hand with the history of white supremacy over nature and the Indigenous people of North America.

In 1882, W. P. Hermann, the Grand Canyon Forest Reserve supervisor, wrote:

> The Grand Canyon of the Colorado River is becoming so renowned for its wonderful and extensive natural Gorge scenery and for its open and clean pine woods, that it should be preserved for the everlasting pleasure and instruction of our intelligent citizens as well as those of foreign countries. Henceforth, I deem it just and necessary to keep the wild and unappreciable Indian off of the reserve.

He was talking about the Havasupai. For centuries until European colonization, much of the land along the Grand Canyon's South Rim was occupied by the Havasupai people, who freely roamed over its 3 million acres. By 1882, the U.S. government had restricted them to a minuscule reservation at the bottom of the canyon. The Havasupai village is one of the most isolated Indian reservations in the United States, accessible only by walking or mules or, for those who can afford it, helicopters. During the summer, the villagers raise crops in the gorge, and during the winter they travel to the canyon's plateaus, where they hunt and graze cattle.

Almost a century later, in 1971, the National Park Service, in collaboration with the Sierra Club, proposed that the Havasupai people should be further restricted. The park had its eye on the plateaus where the Havasupai had permits for winter activities. According to the proposal, "There is

a continuing concern for providing sufficient camping ca-
pacity for tourists who are within and moving through the
region ... Private campgrounds are meeting some of the
demand. Indian reservations offer a great potential for this
and other recreational activities."

On May 18, 1971, the National Park Service held a public
hearing regarding its "Master Plan for Grand Canyon National Park." Without the traditional grazing lands that fell
outside their reservation, the Havasupai would lose whatever economic autonomy they had. But it was not just a
question of income. For the Havasupai, their land is their
body and their spirit. They were not invited to the hear-
ings held to discuss the master plan. Nevertheless, they
showed up to advocate for themselves. Stephen Hirst's book
I Am the Grand Canyon: The Story of the Havasupai People
documents this remarkable moment.

After all the bureaucrats and conservationists had spoken,
Lee Marshall, the Havasupai tribal chairman, addressed the
gathering: "I heard all you people talking about the Grand
Canyon. Well, you're looking at it. I am the Grand Canyon."

Even the Grand Canyon is not the Grand Canyon after all.

Kerala, too, has its own shameful history of committing
violence against Indigenous people, appropriating their
lands, and forcing them into slavery. One of the bloodi-
est incidents took place in Wayanad, about an hour away
from where we were, in the Muthanga forest, the traditional
homeland of many Adivasi groups. Long ousted from the
forest so that it could be converted into a sanctuary, the

Adivasi communities of Muthanga were forced into pen-
ury and landlessness. In 2002, they reentered and occupied
Muthanga. The face-off between the community and the
government ended when eight hundred policemen entered
the forest and opened fire on the fifty-odd Adivasi families.
Only a month before this incident, the government had
organized a summit for foreign investors, where it put up
tourism in Muthanga as an investment opportunity.

From Uluru to the Grand Canyon to Muthanga, the
tourist walks freely through lands that Indigenous people
have been evicted from. This is the superpower of tourism: it can masquerade as a public good while legitimizing
land-grabbing.

•

The ecologist Suprabha Seshan lives and works at the Gurukula Botanical Sanctuary in Wayanad, a forest community focused on rewilding. Seshan has drawn attention to
how forest conservation should go beyond simply increasing
tree cover. Forests are not just trees and tigers. They are ferns
and frogs as well. Seshan and her team have been painstak-
ingly cultivating the biome at the sanctuary, bringing in en-
dangered species of plants from around the Western Ghats
to Gurukula. "We refer to these plants as refugees, similar
to human refugees suffering the depredations of war, dis-
placement, climate change and general toxification of the
environment," she wrote in *Scroll*.

Elsewhere, in an interview, she recalled a conversation

with a visiting Japanese botanist, who marveled at the diversity of Gurukula's forests and compared them to the homogenization of vast areas in his country. I was struck by this comparison—I thought then of all the cities I loved and their tolerance for weirdness. A forest is like a city in its tolerance for the weirdness and wildness of biodiversity. As Kerala filled up with malls and apartment buildings, here in its forest was a final refuge for its most vulnerable inhabitants, a place where poisonous snakes can slither through the undergrowth and cicadas can live and die anonymously, and tigers can have multicourse elephant meals.

•

My thoughts kept circling back to that baby elephant whose skeleton we saw on our first walk. The way its heart must have lurched when it felt the claws of the tiger, the weight of its hunger. And at first, every single one of my thoughts was about feeling sorry for the baby elephant. But then I started weighing the cuteness of baby elephants against the tiger's need to eat. How absurd it is to use the metrics of sympathy to understand this encounter. And even more absurd was whatever it was that made me think my opinion on this was important. Nature is indifferent to the cuteness of baby elephants and the overwrought emotions of biophobes.

One day, while lounging on the veranda, trying and failing not to feel virtuous about "being in nature," I noticed a faint movement. It wasn't a tiger or an elephant. It was a green cricket struggling in one of the spiderwebs hanging delicately from the wooden beam above me. Even as I watched, a wasp swooped in, plucked the cricket out of the web, and carried it off. *How annoyed the spider must be,* I thought, *to have the lunch it worked so hard for so unceremoniously snatched away.*

It dawned on me then that I was waiting and waiting for a grand wildlife sighting—a red-carpet welcome from Mother Nature, a parade of elephants. And it was not going to happen. My forest hikes changed. We walked quietly through the forest, savoring its deep strange silence and the brooding darkness. The more I did not see, the more I felt seen. The animals were there: behind trees, in hollows, under the rocks, watching us. They knew instinctively that their lives depended on not being seen.

Conversely there were all the animals I would like to not see in my everyday life. The roaches that infest a certain generation of New York City apartments, the rats that lurk behind restaurants everywhere in the world, the bony street dogs that skulk at the corners of Indian streets, the mosquitoes that turn outdoor dinners into slapping festivals, the microbes that infect and rot and mold. How strange that I had never thought of them as nature. How strange that I had never thought of myself as nature.

Slowly my fear of nature was turning into awe, a grudging admiration for the forces of life and death that are at work in every tree, for the animals that knew how to be invisible and frustrate us while we walked through their habitats, even, dammit, for the leeches blindly groping their way toward heat, determined to live.

Twelve days after we arrived, the Jeep bumped us back down the road toward the small town at the base of the mountain. We were on our way home. Our driver braked suddenly and pointed across the valley. On the mountain on the other side, an elephant duo was slowly walking down toward a canyon. A mother and a child. They moved slowly, the mother unfurling her trunk to grab at branches and the child imitating her. They were so far away. I screwed up my middle-aged eyes and pointed the animals out to my daughter, wishing we were close enough to . . . to what? To see them better?

Now, you should know that I have seen a lot of elephants. They were a common sight on the streets of Kerala when I was growing up, and even the most fearless trucks and buses would slow down and shrink toward the sides when sharing road space with an elephant. I loved the dignity of it, the elephant calmly striding down the street, indifferent to all of us gazing in awe. Ironically, many of these elephants worked in the logging and sand-mining industries and were used to haul heavy loads. My mother's uncle owned a couple of elephants, who were often hired out like any other livestock. When these elephants were brought to the river to bathe, we children, visiting for summer vacations, would run out to watch, hoping the mahouts were in a good mood and would let the elephants frolic in the waters. Sometimes they were rented by temples for festivals. Even churches and mosques in Kerala would line up a procession of elephants at festival time. The taller the elephants, the longer their trunks, the grander the festival. Some of these celebrity elephants had their own Facebook fan pages.

Yes, I have followed elephants on social media. All this is to say—elephants there have been aplenty in my life.

But these elephants across the valley were the first ones I had seen in their home. And even from this distance, I could tell that the mother elephant, confidently swirling her trunk to reach for leaves, was another species of confidence and grace. Her very gait as she floated among the trees, offering leaves to her child, trumpeting love notes, signaled such a lavish freedom that it was not freedom anymore—it was the fullness of her existence. And it was only when I saw this elephant in the wild that I realized that every elephant I had seen until then was simply putting one foot in front of the other, grimly making its way through life. What I thought was dignity had been mourning.

I felt grateful then that we were not closer. That this elephant and her child could loiter without feeling the human gaze on them. They were in no danger from me and the rest of my species. I hoped for her a long life and I hoped for her freedom from captivity and I hoped for her the great mundane joy of keeping her child alive.

As she walked farther away from us down the canyon, the elephant became smaller and smaller. Soon, in the vast panorama of the valley, she looked like a tiny bug. A leech. Like a leech climbing up a warm leg, the elephant and her child moved, slowly, feeling their way through the mountain, alert and trusting. I felt a soft movement on my own leg and looked down. Predictably, there was a leech climbing up my leg, alert and trusting. To the leech, I was the Grand Canyon.

Chapter

NINE

✈

AS MUCH AS I LOVE TRAINS AND CITY BUSES, MY FAVORITE
form of public transportation is the carousel.

The first time I sat on a painted horse, I felt overcome by
emotion. I was an adult woman in my twenties. As soon as
the organ in the hundred-year-old carousel in Brooklyn's
Prospect Park started playing, there were tears. As my horse
moved, I was, too.

New York City, where I live, has as many as twelve carousels, most of them antique, most of them located in parks.
The one nearest to me is the Prospect Park Carousel, which
contains not only fifty-three hand-carved horses but also a
lion, a giraffe, a deer, and two chariots pulled by dragons.
It was created in 1912 by Charles Carmel, a master carver
of carousels. This was the golden age of the carousel, just
before it ended with the First World War. Since 1912, the
Prospect Park Carousel has gone through many ups and
downs, falling into disuse and mechanical troubles before
eventually being restored.

Going up and down and up and down is a very carousel movement. The horses that move up and down on the
poles with all four feet in the air are called "jumpers." A

carousel may also have "prancers," which have their two front feet in the air, the back two on the ground, as well as "stargazers," which have their heads raised at a forty-five- or ninety-degree angle, as if they are looking skyward.

Carousel history is also full of ups and downs. The carousel started as a war-training game in the thirteenth century. Imagine the moment eight hundred years ago. The Khmer Empire is building Angkor Wat. Tuareg nomads have just founded a trading post called Timbuktu that will soon grow into the cultural capital of West Africa. A boy called Jalaluddin is leaving his home in Balkh to journey to Anatolia in search of a home and learning. And in the Mediterranean, Muslim and Christian soldiers are participating in one of the most intense cultural-exchange programs ever, known as the Crusades. This is how some European crusaders noticed that the Arab and Turkish warriors played a combat game that involved riding around in circles and throwing perfumed clay balls at one another. The idea was that you would catch the ball and throw it at someone else. But if the ball hit you, you left the game and bore the scent for weeks. When the Spanish and Italian soldiers returned to Europe, they brought back coffee, sugar, and this game.

Although, what was Europe? The most glamorous city of the twelfth century was Constantinople, the Byzantine capital, modern-day Istanbul. Europe was a bunch of feudal entities at war with one another, riddled with disease and poverty. Chunks of Spain and Portugal were in Muslim hands. And stretching from Eastern Europe to China, Siberia to South Asia, was the Mongol Empire.

Garosello: This is what the soldiers called the game. In Italian it means *little war*.

What marvelously twisted irony that the empires that the men of the twelfth and thirteenth centuries fought for are gone but the horse-riding game thingy they happened to exchange is still around.

What was a game of skill in the Seljuk Turkish world transformed into pageantry in Italy and France. Riders on lavishly decorated horses performed to music, often in circular arenas, while royals watched. Carousels became a popular tournament event at which knights showed off their horsemanship skills. A simple machine was devised so that they could practice lancing a dangling ring with a sword while riding.

In 1662, a particularly fabulous equine demonstration took place in a public square in Paris to entertain Louis XIV. The square got renamed Place du Carrousel. In 1789, the royal palace at the Place du Carrousel was burned to the ground by members of the Paris Commune.

By the nineteenth century, carousels began to appear at country fairs. They were no longer involved in pageants or tournaments. They had turned into simple machines containing a central post with roughly carved horses and benches made of scrap wood, powered by a single live horse. By the mid-nineteenth century, the live horse was replaced by a hand-cranked machine with various wooden animals on wheels or arms extending from a rotating center post.

Then the steam engine came along. The steam-driven

carousel was just what the country fair of the mid-nineteenth century needed. Trains had made travel far easier than ever before and, in order to stay relevant, the fairs had to offer more spectacle and entertainment. Flush with buying power, the prototypical consumer-tourist of the era was ready to be entertained, and soon carousels became show-cases of engineering skill and imaginative fantasy. They also became bigger and stronger and included multiple rows of animals, and they began moving to music. The festive calli-ope music of the carousel started ringing out at the seaside resorts that were mushrooming in Europe.

The steam engine also powered the ships that were sail-ing across the oceans with immigrants. One of those immi-grants was Gustav Dentzel, a young German woodworker, who sailed down the Rhine and across the Atlantic to the shores of the United States with the parts of a carousel in the hold of the steamboat. Over the next fifty years what was once a Turkish military-combat game became a full-scale popular entertainment in North America.

An idea for a novel that I don't have time to write: how Gustav Dentzel, a twenty-year-old furniture-maker from Kreuznach, Germany, who landed in the United States just as the Ottoman Empire was beginning its slow cookie crumble, would go on to establish a carousel empire on the East Coast.

Opening scene of this novel: Dentzel is in Richmond, Virginia, with a simple carousel he is testing out on the American market. It consists of a few benches suspended from chains. So far it has been a hit at the many fairgrounds he has taken it to. But in Richmond, the town's boys throw stones at him and insult him. Why? He does not understand. His feelings are hurt.

It is the local police who explain to him that playing "Marching Through Georgia," a Union song of the Civil War, as the musical accompaniment for his carousel is not the path to popularity in the American South. It is a mistake Dentzel will never make again. He is not only an expert wood-carver; he is also an entrepreneur.

Country fairs are in his blood. In Germany, his family would travel around fairs during the summer and retreat to their town to carve carousel animals during the winter. But unlike in Europe, carousels are rare in the United States. Dentzel sets up G. A. Dentzel, Steam and Horsepower Carousel Builder in Germantown, Philadelphia.

The Carousel Museum in Bristol, Connecticut, has faithfully replicated an early-twentieth-century carousel workshop. Pasted on the wall of the workshop is the master carver's drawing. The drawing was important because many of the immigrant carvers did not speak English. Dentzel's drawings were probably sketched in charcoal, either directly on the wall or on large sheets of paper in his workshop.

Dentzel's workshop was always a welcoming place for immigrant carvers. My favorite story is that of Salvatore Cernigliaro, a twenty-three-year-old from Palermo, who arrived in the United States in 1902 "full of energy and corragio," as he described it in a letter. Cerni, as he would come to be known, made his living as a wood-carver, but the work was never reliable. One day, down on his luck and unemployed, he went to meet Dentzel and mustered all his English and said to him: "Me, wood-carver, job?"

Dentzel spoke to him in German, and Cerni understood that there was no work for him. He went away disappointed. A week later, hungry and tired, he was praying at Saint Stefano Church in Germantown. "Mr. Lord, I have only $4 in my pocket—it is my last pay for board and if I don't find a job now, they will throw me out," he wrote later about his prayer.

After he prayed, he felt thirsty. He remembered then that there was a well in the courtyard of Dentzel's workshop nearby. So he went to drink water there. He met Dentzel again, who invited him inside. Inside the workshop there was a Tyrolean immigrant who could manage a few words of Italian. "Why didn't you come last week?" he asked Cerni. Dentzel had offered him a job then, but Cerni had misunderstood.

Dentzel and Cerni were part of an influx of skilled and eager European craftspeople eager to make their way. The Danish immigrant Charles I. D. Looff worked in a furniture factory in New York, and at night, with scrap wood brought home from his job, he began carving carousel animals in his apartment. Looff opened the first carousel at the trolley park in Coney Island.

The trolley parks were so named because they were at the end of trolley lines. They were recreation areas, with Ferris wheels and swimming pools, roller coasters, and games and boat rides. Many of them were constructed by the trolley companies themselves, to increase their revenues by luring people to ride to the end of the lines on the weekends and holidays. There were hundreds of trolley parks in the United States before the First World War—some of these turned into permanent amusement parks.

Over the next fifty years, carousel maestros would create roughly four thousand carousels. American carousels were much larger than their European predecessors. Many of them were populated with fantastic creatures unheard of in European carousels. While European carousels ran clockwise, American carousels ran counterclockwise, as if to say pointedly, look, we are going in another direction. But, in one respect, carousels did not change: they brought with them the fairground music of Europe.

Carousel music is often called the happiest music in the world. In February 2021, the satirical newspaper *The Onion* headlined: "If It Weren't For Covid, You'd Be On A Carousel Right Now." Quoting a fictitious report by the United Nations Development Programme, *The Onion* wrote: "We found irrefutable evidence that in a hypothetical scenario in which the coronavirus outbreak has never occurred, a gentle breeze blows through your hair, the smell of freshly popped popcorn wafts through a park, you're seated on a beautiful historic merry-go-round, and you're truly, truly happy."

For years now, since my first carousel ride, I have wondered about this happiness, the way it is a shorthand for the complex of feelings that surge in me when I ride a carousel. I have fumbled through the felt senses and muscle memories of my body. This rush in my heart, this feeling of being alive, the way the rhythms inside me and outside me are in sync. This is the closest I have come to understanding the carousel emotion—belonging; be-longing.

Fairground organ music belongs to the nineteenth century. For centuries before, pipe organs had provided music in the cathedrals and courts of Europe. But in the decades in between the final dissolution of the Ottoman Empire and the Berlin Conference, organ music wandered out of palaces and places of worship and into dance halls, streets, and fairgrounds, where it turned into a loud and mechanized secular symphony. It became louder and faster because it had to work harder to cut through the clutter of carnival noise.

It seems to me that carousel music has never quite moved outside this time warp. It captures a moment in time when everyday life stood poised to be transformed. Already the forces of capitalism and colonialism were at work, and machines would be put to their service. But here in this brief bubble of time, machines had made life easier, and time itself was more plentiful. For a few moments in history, we had machines but they didn't have us.

It is from the cultural and social ferment of this moment that modern tourism emerged. This is why the carousel is a perfect metaphor for tourism in all its seductions and complications. What is a metaphor, after all? In Athens, the mass transit system is called Metaforas. *Meta* means "across"; *phero* means "carry." A metaphor is a form of transportation, whether in place or in meaning. The carousel is a metaphor in more ways than one.

Like a modern tourist, the carousel rider moves in a tightly circumscribed circle. There is nothing new to see or hear, whether it's the Grand Tour or the hajj, whether it's the backpacker trail or the walking tour. Yet every time the music begins and my horse starts moving, I forget that it is not going anywhere. The Earth spins thousands of kilometers per hour, but we do not feel it because we, too, are spinning. Who is to say what movement is?

Carousels also remind me that we live in a multi-temporal world, that history will compost itself. We know this. But we keep this knowledge at the edge. We divide our stories into eras, and we imagine we have come so far from our ancestors. But when I am riding a painted wooden horse dancing around a centrifugal axis, this knowledge surges in, so forcefully that it is not even awareness; it is pure consciousness.

This meeting of mystery and materiality is also why I look forward to airport carousels. Once, at a baggage carousel in Istanbul, where some of my fellow passengers were returning from the hajj, I saw a box of zamzam water and a box of whiskey, both marked fragile, coming down the carousel together. The carousel handles with care these contradictions. The profound and the profane in one perfect circle.

Every circle of the carousel is just that—one perfect circle. Then it is gone forever. Look, the man who was sitting outside on the grass reading a book is gone now. A bird takes off from a tree and the world will never be the same again. The café where you were once young is now a phone store. The museum is a mosque. The elephant's bones have become mushroom. Where one empire has dissolved into nothing, another rises.

When we travel, we are not moving from place to place. We are moving from one moment in time to another moment in time. We are tricking ourselves into paying attention to the thing that is hardest to pay attention to. On the carousel and on the tourist trail, it is time that reveals itself. The present does not exist. Only the past and the future do. But on the border between those two, a border that is thinner than a hair, sharper than a sword's edge, there is a moment. To call it the present would be to overstate it. But it is there: a microworld of galloping horses, overheard conversations, and bits of song. There is no now but now.

I CALL IT THE THIRD WORLD BECAUSE NONE OF ITS other names do justice to it. Third World, like the third eye, is another kind of knowing. Sure, we can call it "developing countries," we can call it "emerging economies," we can call it the postcolonial world, we can call it the Global South. (But Australia?) If we were being absolutely honest, wouldn't we just call it the exploited world? Still—the irresistible know-ingness of "Third World." How extra it is. How it propels you beyond primaries and binaries. The audacity of its un-wieldy internal rhyme. Its elasticity that has made space for so many meanings, from varying degrees of nonalignment to varying shades of melanin. The way these meanings are piled one on top of the other, like its buildings, the Internet café on top of the hardware shop on top of the supermarket. The überness of its cities, the way they sprawl from year to year, their centers constantly shifting, changing downtowns as if they were shoes. Those enormous roundabouts, often dreamed up by some long-forgotten colonial planner; the way traffic will pause at a red light, like a wild beast still-ing itself before a pounce. The streets without WALK signs where you have to collect a crowd and find a momentary imagined community before you cross them. All the things that are sold on sidewalks: cheap toys, pirated books, phone chargers, flowers. All the forms of transportation that have evolved to fill in the gaps: cycle rickshaws, scooter taxis, autos, dolla vans, tuk-tuks, TikTok. All the broken languages that are spoken at its petrol stations and junctions, where slang passes from one tongue to another like a communion. The back alleys of its cities and towns, where backgammon games and drug deals and export-surplus shops and revolution planning hang out side by side. The stubbornness of its villages, where ancestral eyebrows regard plastic-wrapped vegetables and other forms of modernity skeptically. The way its people, in Addis and Phnom Penh and Delhi, can fix anything mechanical with some glue and a wire and five minutes, making development sustainable before sustainable was plastic-wrapped into Sustainable. The Third World is a world of koans and contradictions where there is no god but there is god. A world so small that so many of us carry it around everywhere, rolling its borders out like a paratha/porotta/farata/palata/buss-up-shut. A world so big we don't have to go back where we came from because we are already there. We learn to look for it wherever we go; we recognize its chaos and its creativity in the bad neighborhoods and banlieues and inner cities and overcrowded public schools and projects and the wrong side of the tracks in the First World countries we have migrated to, even when those countries keep shrugging and laughing about First World problems, as if no one outside the United States or Europe or Canada has ever had to choose between two different kinds of moisturizers or wines or fonts or whatever. To speak of the Third World is to bring it into being, piled on top of the other worlds but out of reach, almost invisible, blurred by traffic fumes and a bad reputation, except to those of us who grew up t/here. It's not offensive to me. How can it be, when my soul is a Third World country? Its nasty women, bad hombres, and shitholes are dear to me. Third World Third World Third World.

ACKNOWLEDGMENTS

The New York Foundation for the Arts, Café Royal Cultural Foundation, I-Park Foundation, and Salty Quill Writers' Retreat made the writing of this book possible with gifts of money and time and space.

So much gratitude to my agent, David Godwin, and Lisette Verhagen for championing this book before it was a book.

At Catapult, Megha Majumdar's brilliant vision gave this book shape and momentum. Laura Gonzalez's faith in this book was so infectious it infected even me. Summer Farah brought tough questions and fire emojis, and Alicia Kroell took it all to the finishing line with infinite patience. My thanks also to the production team, led by Wah-Ming Chang.

Arpita Das, Rollo Romig, Sebene Selassie, and Raksha Vasudevan read drafts and gave freely of their fierce intelligence and critical insights. This book has also benefited greatly from conversations with Rajesh Chavda, Sina Fabian, Minal Hajratwala, Ana Laura Martinez, Kalathmika Natarajan, Enrique Salmon, Kate Sekules, Steven Tagle, Robert Young, and Paul Zacharia. Thanks also to Fatemeh

Keshavarz, who graciously permitted me to use her translation of the opening lines of *The Mathnawi*.

Knowing that Zarine Habeeb and Liz Romig are tapping their fingers waiting to read this book has meant so much to me. Thank you, sisters, for being the gentlest of gentle readers. All my heart to my favorite aisle and middle seat passengers, Rollo Romig and Sophya Habib Romig.

SELECT BIBLIOGRAPHY

CHAPTER ONE

Baedeker, Karl. *Italy, from the Alps to Naples*. Karl Baedeker, 1904.

Becker, Elizabeth. *Overbooked: The Exploding Business of Travel and Tourism*. Simon & Schuster, 2016.

Christie, Agatha, writing as Mary Westmacott. *Absent in the Spring*. Collins, 1973.

Dalrymple, William. "What Goes Round . . ." *The Guardian*, November 5, 2005.

Forster, E. M. *A Room with a View*. Edward Arnold, 1908.

Friend, Tad. "The Parachute Artist." *The New Yorker*, April 18, 2005.

Grimshaw, Mike. *Bibles and Baedekers: Tourism, Travel, Exile and God*. Taylor & Francis, 2014.

Hajratwala, Minal. *Moon Fiji*. Avalon Publishing, 2019.

MacLean, Rory. *Magic Bus: On the Hippie Trail from Istanbul to India*. Viking, 2006.

Mendelson, Edward. "Baedeker's Universe." *Yale Review* 74 (Spring 1985), 386–403.

Parsons, Nicholas T. *Worth the Detour: A History of the Guidebook*. History Press, 2007.

Rumi, Jalal al-Din. From *The Mathnawi*, translated by Fatemeh Keshavarz, by correspondence.

Vail, Pegi, dir. *Gringo Trails*. Icarus Films, 2013.

CHAPTER TWO

Becker, Elizabeth. *Overbooked: The Exploding Business of Travel and Tourism*. Simon & Schuster, 2016.

Chambers, William and Robert Chambers, eds. *Chambers's Pocket Miscellany*, vol. 5. Edinburgh: W. & R. Chambers, 1852.

Endy, Christopher. *Cold War Holidays: American Tourism in France*. University of North Carolina Press, 2005.

Jovanović, Srđan. "Passportism: Xenophobia from Discourse to Policy." Available at SSRN: ssrn.com/abstract=2930877.

Khair, Tabish. "The Colour of Our Passports." *The Hindu Magazine*. December 21, 2003.

Lalami, Laila. *Conditional Citizens: On Belonging in America*. Knopf Doubleday, 2020.

Levenstein, Harvey. *We'll Always Have Paris: American Tourists in France Since 1930*. University of Chicago Press, 2004.

Lloyd, Martin. *The Passport: The History of Man's Most Travelled Document*. Sutton, 2003.

Mongia, Radhika. *Indian Migration and Empire: A Colonial Genealogy of the Modern State*. Duke University Press, 2018.

Natarajan, Kalathmika. "The Privilege of the Indian Passport (1947–1967): Caste, Class and the Afterlives of Indenture in Indian Diplomacy." *Modern Asian Studies* 57, Issue 2 (March 2023): 321–50.

Recchi, Ettore, Emanuel Deutschmann, Lorenzo Gabrielli, and Nodira Khomatova. "The Global Visa Cost Divide: How and Why the Price for Travel Permits Varies World-wide." *Political Geography* 86, 2021.

Robertson, Craig. *The Passport in America: The History of a Document*. Oxford University Press, 2010.

Sen, Amartya. "Demeaning a Nobelist," interview by Louis Uchitelle. *The New York Times*, February 7, 1999.

Torpey, John. *The Invention of Passport: Surveillance, Citizenship and the State*. Cambridge University Press, 2000.

CHAPTER THREE

Cavafy, C. P. "The City," in *Sixty-Three Poems*. Translated by J. C. Cavafy. Athens: Ikaros, 2003.

D'Eramo, Marco. *The World in a Selfie: An Inquiry into the Tourist Age*. Verso Books, 2021.

Lévi-Strauss, Claude. *Tristes Tropiques*. Translated by John Russell. Atheneum, 1961.

MacCannell, Dean. *The Tourist: A New Theory of the Leisure Class*. 1976. University of California Press, 1999.

Moser, Benjamin. "The Alienist." *The New Yorker*, July 9 and 16, 2018.

Nandy, Ashis. "Defining a New Cosmopolitanism: Towards a Dialogue of Asian Civilisations." In *Trajectories: Inter-Asia Cultural Studies*, edited by Kuan-Hsing Chen, 142–49. London: Routledge, 1998.

CHAPTER FOUR

Appadurai, Arjun. "Street Culture." *The Oxford Anthology*

of the Modern Indian City, Volume 1: The City in Its Plenitude, edited by Vinay Lal. Oxford University Press, 2013.

Bay, Mia. *Traveling Black: A Story of Race and Resistance.* Harvard University Press, 2021.

Elkin, Lauren. *Flâneuse: Women Walk the City in Paris, New York, Tokyo, Venice, and London.* Random House, 2016.

Kerouac, Jack. *On the Road.* Viking Press, 1957.

Least Heat-Moon, William. *Blue Highways: A Journey into America.* Gale, 1983.

Moskin, Julia. "Food Trucks in Paris? U.S. Cuisine Finds Open Minds, and Mouths." *The New York Times,* June 4, 2012.

Nead, Lynda. *Victorian Babylon: People, Streets and Images in Nineteenth-Century London.* Yale University Press, 2000.

Phadke, Shilpa, Sameera Khan, and Shilpa Ranade. *Why Loiter?: Women and Risk on Mumbai Streets.* Penguin Books, 2011.

Rankine, Claudia. *Citizen.* Minneapolis: Graywolf Press, 2014.

CHAPTER FIVE

Dunn, Ross E. *The Adventures of Ibn Battuta: A Muslim Traveler of the Fourteenth Century.* University of California Press, 2012.

Fernández-Armesto, Felipe. *Pathfinders: A Global History of Exploration.* W. W. Norton, 2007.

Ghosh, Amitav. *The Nutmeg's Curse: Parables for a Planet in Crisis.* University of Chicago Press, 2022.

Gibbon, Edward. *The History of the Decline and Fall of the*

Roman Empire, Volume IV. London: Strahan & Cadell, 1788.

Gosch, Stephen, and Peter Stearns. *Premodern Travel in World History.* Taylor & Francis, 2007.

Khair, Tabish, ed. *Other Routes: 1500 Years of African and Asian Travel Writing.* Signal, 2006.

Legassie, Shayne. *The Medieval Invention of Travel.* University of Chicago Press, 2017.

Paniker, Ayyappa. *Indian Narratology.* Indira Gandhi National Centre for the Arts, 2003.

Ravenstein, E. G., translator. *A Journal of the First Voyage of Vasco da Gama, 1497–1499.* Bedford Press, 1898.

Reader, Ian. *Pilgrimage: A Very Short Introduction.* Oxford University Press, 2015.

Zuelow, Eric. *A History of Modern Tourism.* Bloomsbury Publishing, 2015.

CHAPTER SIX

Adams, Percy G. *Travelers and Travel Liars, 1660–1800.* Northwestern University, 1962.

Forna, Aminatta. *The Window Seat: Notes from a Life in Motion.* Grove/Atlantic, 2022.

Ghosh, Amitav, introduction. *Other Routes: 1500 Years of African and Asian Travel Writing,* edited by Tabish Khair. Signal, 2006.

Holland, Patrick, and Graham Huggan. *Tourists with Typewriters.* University of Michigan Press, 1998.

Kesavan, Mukul. *The Ugliness of the Indian Male and Other Propositions.* Black Kite, 2008.

Kimmerer, Robin Wall. *Braiding Sweetgrass*. Penguin Books, 2020.

Kincaid, Jamaica, introduction. *Robinson Crusoe*, by Daniel Defoe. Restless Books, 2019.

Lack, H. Walter. "The Discovery, Naming and Typification of Bougainvillea Spectabilis (Nyctaginaceae)." *Willdenowia* 42, no. 1 (2012): 117–26.

Lê, Việt, and Michelle Dizon. *White Gaze*. Chicago: Candor Arts, 2018.

North, Anna, and Kainaz Amira. "National Geographic Faced Up to Its Racist Past. Did It Actually Get Better?" *Vox*, May 6, 2021.

Pratt, Mary Louise. *Imperial Eyes: Travel Writing and Transculturation*. Taylor & Francis, 2003.

Ridley, Glynis. *The Discovery of Jeanne Baret: A Story of Science, the High Seas, and the First Woman to Circumnavigate the Globe*. Crown, 2010.

Said, Edward. *Orientalism*. Pantheon Books, 1978.

Seale, Yasmin, foreword. *The Book of Travels*, by Antun Yusuf Hanna Diyab. New York University Press, 2021.

CHAPTER SEVEN

Austen, Jane. *Sanditon*. Davies, 1975.

Bahadur, Gaiutra. *Coolie Woman: The Odyssey of Indenture*. Hurst, 2013.

Beckert, Sven. *Empire of Cotton: A Global History*. Knopf Doubleday Publishing Group, 2014.

Broadberry, Stephen, and Bishnupriya Gupta. "Cotton Textiles and the Great Divergence: Lancashire, India and

Shifting Competitive Advantage, 1600-1850." London: Centre for Economic Policy Research, 2005.

Carroll, Lewis. *Alice's Adventures in Wonderland.* Macmillan, 1865.

Griffiths, Jay. *Wild: An Elemental Journey.* Penguin Books, 2007.

Isserman, Maurice, and Stewart Weaver. *Fallen Giants: A History of Himalayan Mountaineering from the Age of Empire to the Age of Extremes.* Yale University Press, 2008.

Karuka, Manu. *Empire's Tracks: Indigenous Nations, Chinese Workers, and the Transcontinental Railroad.* University of California Press, 2019.

Kennedy, Dane. *The Magic Mountains: Hill Stations and the British Raj.* University of California Press, 1996.

Lisle, Debbie. *The Global Politics of Contemporary Travel Writing.* Cambridge University Press, 2006.

Mintz, Sidney. *Sweetness and Power: The Place of Sugar in Modern History.* Penguin Publishing Group, 1986.

Munson, James, and Richard Mullen. *The Smell of the Continent: The British Discover Europe.* Pan Macmillan, 2010.

Osborne, Lawrence. *The Naked Tourist: In Search of Adventure and Beauty in the Age of the Airport Mall.* Farrar, Straus and Giroux, 2007.

Osnos, Evan. "The Grand Tour." *The New Yorker,* April 18, 2011.

Rediker, Marcus. *The Slave Ship: A Human History.* Penguin Publishing Group, 2007.

Riello, Giorgio. *Cotton: The Fabric that Made the Modern World*. Cambridge University Press, 2015.

Schultz, Kai, Jeffrey Gettleman, Mujib Mashal, and Bhadra Sharma. "'It Was Like a Zoo': Death on an Unruly, Overcrowded Everest." *The New York Times*, May 26, 2019.

Singh, Bhasha. *Unseen: The Truth About Manual Scavenging*. Translated by Reenu Talwar. Penguin Books, 2014.

Solnit, Rebecca. *Wanderlust: A History of Walking*. Penguin Publishing Group, 2001.

Urry, John. *The Tourist Gaze: Leisure and Travel in Contemporary Societies*. Sage Publications, 2002.

Verne, Jules. *Around the World in Eighty Days*, translated by George Makepeace Towle. Sampson Low, 1874.

Wilson, Bee. *Sandwich: A Global History*. Reaktion Books, 2010.

Zuelow, Eric. *A History of Modern Tourism*. Bloomsbury Publishing, 2015.

CHAPTER EIGHT

Daly, Natasha. "Suffering Unseen: The Dark Truth Behind Wildlife Tourism." *National Geographic*, June 2019.

Deming, Alison H., and Lauret E. Savoy. *The Colors of Nature: Culture, Identity, and the Natural World*. Milkweed Editions, 2011.

Gadgil, Madhav. "Sacred Groves: An Ancient Tradition of Nature Conservation." *Scientific American*, December 1, 2018.

Hirst, Stephen. *I Am the Grand Canyon: The Story of the Havasupai People*. Grand Canyon Association, 2006.

Riederer, Rachel. "Barry Lopez and the Innocence of Boomer Travel Writing." *The Nation*, May 30, 2019.

Seshan, Suprabha. "An Ancient Rainforest in Kerala Teaches Us What We're Losing Out On in Our Lonely Cities of Concrete." *Scroll*, February 4, 2018.

Walther, Sundhya. *Multispecies Modernity: Disorderly Life in Postcolonial Literature*. Wilfrid Laurier University Press, 2021.

White, Evelyn C. "Black Women and the Wilderness." In *The Stories that Shape Us: Contemporary Women Write About the West*, edited by Teresa Jordan and James Hepworth, 376–83. New York: Norton, 1995.

CHAPTER NINE

Hinds, Anne Dion. *Grab the Brass Ring: The American Carousel*. Crown Publishers, 1990.

"Report: If It Weren't for Covid, You'd Be on a Carousel Right Now." *The Onion*, February 9, 2021.

Weedon, Geoff, and Richard Ward. *Fairground Art: The Art Forms of Travelling Fairs, Carousels and Carnival Midways*. Abbeville Press, 1982.

SHAHNAZ HABIB is a writer and translator based in Brooklyn. She translates from her mother tongue, the south Indian language of Malayalam, and has translated two novels, *Jasmine Days*, winner of the 2018 JCB Prize, and *Al Arabian Novel Factory*. *Airplane Mode* is her first book.